Praise for *Infinite Awakening*

"With deep clarity and a heart attuned to our shared humanity, Stephan Bodian illuminates a path to freedom and love that feels both timeless and intimately grounded and alive."

—Tara Brach, author of *Radical Acceptance* and *True Refuge*

"Stephan Bodian is a master teacher sharing a lifetime of realizations and exquisitely skillful guidance, with both deep insights and powerful experiential practices. With a kind smile he invites us to come home, in the experiencing beyond all understanding, to a natural resting in awareness, love, and inner peace."

—Rick Hanson, PhD, author of *Buddha's Brain*, *Hardwiring Happiness*, *Resilient*, and *Neurodharma*

"Stephan Bodian offers a tender, clear, compassionate, and beautifully articulated guide to the timeless understanding that lies at the heart of all true spirituality."

—Rupert Spira, author of *The Nature of Consciousness* and *Being Aware of Being Aware*

"Having read many books in this field, I can say that *Infinite Awakening* will be at the top of my recommended reading list for students. Stephan's beautiful writing opens doorways to the infinite and intimate exploration of who we truly are while addressing the roadblocks and challenging emotions we meet along the way."

—Loch Kelly, author of *Shift into Freedom* and *The Way of Effortless Mindfulness*

"*Infinite Awakening* is a wise, nuanced, warm-hearted, honest, and beautifully written distillation of living insight into the open-ended nature of nondual spiritual awakening. Stephan Bodian clearly points to and evokes our undivided nature while creatively addressing the psychological challenges of trauma, eros, and intimate relationship."

—John J. Prendergast, PhD, author of *Your Deepest Ground* and *The Deep Heart*

"*Infinite Awakening* is both a comprehensive map for understanding the nondual path and a treasure chest of practical meditations, pointers, and wise advice. But most remarkably, it's a portal through which to discover ourselves *as* pure presence. A must-read for anyone longing to taste the fullest nectar of life."

—Nancy Colier, author of *Can't Stop Thinking* and *The Emotionally Exhausted Woman*

"*Infinite Awakening* is a concise but thorough compendium of the primary approaches to the groundless ground of awakening that we all share, and so often don't know how to find. It's a book that had to be written, at this time of growing interest in true awakening, and Stephan's training in several spiritual traditions, as well as psychotherapy, and above all his own deep experience and his skill as a writer, make him ideally placed to provide it."

—Henry Shukman, Zen teacher and author of *Original Love* and *One Blade of Grass*

"A marvelously practical and sensible guide to the process of spiritual awakening. With great clarity, Stephan Bodian distills the essence from a variety of spiritual traditions and crystalizes the wisdom of a lifetime of spiritual exploration."

—Steve Taylor, PhD, author of *The Leap* and *Extraordinary Awakenings*

"A seasoned spiritual teacher and psychotherapist, Stephan Bodian artfully blends psychological insights with timeless spiritual teachings, offering a compassionate and accessible path to liberation. This book is an invitation to shed limiting beliefs and awaken to boundless peace and clarity."

—Lama Palden Drolma, Buddhist teacher and author of *Love on Every Breath*

"An articulate and comprehensive guide to seeing through and working with what brings forth unnecessary suffering. Stephan draws from Eastern spiritual traditions, Western psychology, and his own direct observations and insights to provide a richly textured, multidimensional approach to being alive."

—Joan Tollifson, author of *Nothing to Grasp* and *Death: The End of Self-Improvement*

"Stephan Bodian has devoted his life to exploring what it means and what it takes to recognize who we truly are, and to live wisely and well in this challenging world. This multifaceted book makes his many hard-won discoveries and gentle wisdom available to us all."

—Roger Walsh, MD, PhD, professor at the University of California and cohost of the podcast *Deep Transformation: Self-Society-Spirit*

"I believe this book will become a classic, essential reading for anyone who wishes to practice, experience, or teach the truth of the non-dual. Stephan's clear and nuanced writing is informed by his knowledge gained as a therapist as well as by the wisdom revealed through decades of deep spiritual inquiry and practice in the Zen, Advaita, and Dzogchen traditions."

—Jan Chozen Bays, MD, Zen teacher and author of *How to Train a Wild Elephant* and *Mindful Medicine*

Infinite Awakening

Infinite Awakening

A Guide to Nondual Wisdom and the Pathless Path

STEPHAN BODIAN

Foreword by Adyashanti

SHAMBHALA

Shambhala Publications, Inc.
2129 13th Street
Boulder, Colorado 80302
www.shambhala.com

Epigraph on page v from Stephen Mitchell, ed., *The Enlightened Heart: An Anthology of Sacred Poetry* (HarperCollins, 1993). Translated by the editor. Used with permission of the publisher.

Cover and interior design: Meredith Jarrett

9 8 7 6 5 4 3 2 1

First Edition
Printed in the United States of America

Shambhala Publications makes every effort to print on acid-free, recycled paper.
Shambhala Publications is distributed worldwide by Penguin Random House, Inc., and its subsidiaries.

Library of Congress Cataloging-in-Publication Data
Names: Bodian, Stephan author
Title: Infinite awakening: a guide to nondual wisdom and the pathless path / Stephan Bodian.
Description: First edition. | Boulder, Colorado: Shambhala, [2026] | Includes bibliographical references.
Identifiers: LCCN 2025029329 | ISBN 9781645474722 trade paperback
Subjects: LCSH: Spiritual life | Meditation | Self-consciousness (Awareness) | Whole and parts (Philosophy) | Duality (Logic)
Classification: LCC BL624 .B595 2026
LC record available at https://lccn.loc.gov/2025029329

The authorized representative in the EU for product safety and compliance is eucomply OÜ, Pärnu mnt 139b-14, 11317 Tallinn, Estonia, hello@eucompliancepartner.com.

One instant is eternity
eternity is the now.
When you see through this one instant,
you see through the one who sees.

—Wu-men

Contents

Foreword by Adyashanti ix

Introduction: Nondual Wisdom and the Pathless Path 1

Chapter 1: What Does Spiritual Awakening Really Mean? 9

Meditation: Who Am I? 23

Chapter 2: The Stages of Awakening 27

Meditation: Waking into the Nondual 43

Chapter 3: Preparing the Path 47

Meditation: Global Awareness 64

Chapter 4: The Direct Approach 67

Meditation: Effortless Mindfulness—Rest and Allow 94

Chapter 5: Why Bother with a Teacher? 97

Meditation: Is Anything Missing? 116

Chapter 6: Deconstructing the Dream 119

Meditation: Investigating Your Thoughts 145

Chapter 7: Welcoming What Is 149

Meditation: Welcoming Difficult Emotions 168

Chapter 8: The Impact of Trauma 171

Meditation: Innate Perfection 192

Chapter 9: Awakening Relationship 195

Meditation: Deepening the Connection 219

Chapter 10: Infinite Awakening, Endless Unfolding 221

Meditation: Into the Mystery 229

Acknowledgments 233

Notes 235

Additional Resources 241

About the Author 245

Foreword

There is a spiritual potency within each and every one of us. It is not Buddhist, Christian, Jewish, or Hindu; it is prior to all systems of thought, more prior than can be imagined. It has been given many names throughout history, but the ground of the innermost within has no name. For it is the place where all names come from—yours, mine, ours, theirs. And within this spiritual potency, within this ground of one's being, is a drive to awaken to our true being, reality, or God. It is the whisper of something uncontained, unpredictable, perhaps even dangerous to all that is inauthentic within us. It is the call to the real and the true beyond mere ideas, beliefs, and speculation. It is the sacred endeavoring to awaken to itself, *within and as each of us.* And that means you! In this sense each one of us has a sacred task—to help the sacred become fully conscious of itself within and through this human incarnation. This is quite literally what the book you are reading right now is all about.

I have known Stephan Bodian for over twenty-five years as a spiritual teacher and friend. Not only does he have a rich spiritual background in both Zen Buddhism and Advaita Vedanta, he has a keen understanding of the human psyche. As a psychotherapist for many years, as well as a teacher, he has had a close-up view of what it is to root the psyche in spirit. He has reconnected countless individuals to their essential nature in and as spirit and coached them to beautifully express their unique qualities of spirit in daily life, in their humanity. Stephan understands that reuniting with one's true nature as spirit heals division and brings wholeness to the psyche, enabling individuals to find themselves at home in their own unique autonomy.

Stephan's experience, training, and expertise make him a wise guide who offers grounded, well-tried, and well-informed counsel. *Infinite Awakening* is a guidebook that spans the whole arc of navigating the great complexities of human life as well as the lesser-known terrains of spiritual awakening and the embodiment of deep spiritual insight.

It seems to me that we often look at spiritual awakening in far too narrow a context. When we start on the path, we quite naturally look to our spirituality to help us resolve all manner of personal issues: how to be at peace, manage stress, be more loving, have more connection with the sacred, etc. These are primarily ego-driven wants and desires, and while they are perfectly natural concerns of the ego, when they begin to dominate one's spiritual quest, they eventually limit its unfolding because our true being lies completely beyond the ego.

Indeed, the authentic awakening drive arises from universal impulses and intuitions functioning and moving through the individual more than originating from the individual. The awakening drive is present and functioning at every level of being, even our most human. In fact, we are often most in touch with the awakening drive when we are at our most open and vulnerable as human beings.

The reality of you shines before, during, and after the you who you learned to be. It has no face, no name, no history, no ideology, no dogma, and no argument. But it can appear as all of those guises or none of them. In fact, it isn't an "it" at all. It is the faceless presence that you see in every face, the sentient consciousness that you meet in every pair of eyes looking back at you. It is the you in "you" that is also the you in them.

What you are picks its way like water through life's endless challenges and complexities waiting for a moment, an instant perhaps, when it can remind us once again of the immense mystery that lies deep within us and all around us. For the sacred is not hidden in any way. Rather it is we who hide from it, by clinging to our thoughts, self-image, dogma, and memories, including our religious and spiritual thoughts.

What you are deep down in your roots, before and beyond your individuality, is the cosmos—aware and conscious of itself as the unfathomable mystery that it is. All made possible by the consciousness that is woven throughout the cosmos and livingly present in and as each and every one of us simple human beings. Imagine that!

—Adyashanti

Infinite Awakening

Introduction

Nondual Wisdom and the Pathless Path

Throughout the world's spiritual and religious traditions, hidden beneath the differences in beliefs, customs, rituals, and culture, runs a deep esoteric current of nondual wisdom known as the perennial philosophy. First identified by Western philosophers in the European Renaissance and popularized in the last century by Aldous Huxley, René Guénon, and Huston Smith, this current teaches that there is a limitless, ineffable, and unqualifiable ultimate Ground that expresses itself in, and is not separate from, the relative world of manifestation (everyday reality), and that our final end and purpose as human beings is to recognize this groundless Ground as our true identity.

This current of wisdom runs closest to the surface in the nondual traditions of Asia, particularly Advaita Vedanta, Kashmir Shaivism, Tibetan Dzogchen, and East Asian Zen (Chan). Since the early twentieth century, and especially in the past sixty to seventy years, these teachings have had a major influence on spirituality in the West through the roshis, rinpoches, swamis, and sages (and their books) who have offered successive generations of spiritual seekers a more accessible alternative to the nondual wisdom that's more deeply buried in the dualistic Abrahamic religions long prevalent here.

The universality of this current, and its tendency to keep resurfacing, even in the most challenging circumstances, suggests that it may be hardwired into our DNA and deeply programmed in our nervous systems and need merely be tapped into rather than cultivated or fabricated. In this view, nondual awareness or presence is our natural state, our birthright as human beings, and we just need to turn toward it, recognize it, and let it transform our accustomed way of seeing things from the inside. This recognition is known as spiritual awakening. As my Advaita teacher Jean Klein often said, the seeker is the sought—you already are what you are seeking. You can never get any closer to what you are, you can only be it. This paradox appears in many of the world's spiritual traditions as the parable of the prodigal son or daughter who sets off looking for some distant treasure, only to end up discovering that it's been hidden all along in their own heart(h).

Known as the pathless path, this paradoxical approach calls on us to follow it from the depths of our being but ultimately goes nowhere but right here and now. The rediscovery of our natural state may seem to be our responsibility alone as seekers of truth, but in fact truth itself may be actively seeking to realize, actualize, and recognize itself through each of us. The Sufis, for example, teach that God is a hidden treasure that created human beings so it could know itself. Or, as one anonymous sage put it, that which you are seeking is always seeking you. As the chick, the seeker, pecks to break out of the egg from inside, the mother bird—truth, in the form of the teacher and life circumstances—pecks from outside to release it, in a concerted movement toward greater liberation.

Like the perennial philosophy, the pathless path is an expedient way of talking about what appears to be a universal phenomenon that cuts across cultures and deep into the heart of what it means to be human. Many of you reading this book were drawn to this journey by a deep and ineffable calling of the heart or soul prompted by suffering or curiosity or a yearning to be free of limitations. Yet you were only drawn here because you somehow already recognized the truth in these teachings and already knew the destination as your very own true self. In the words of T. S. Eliot from his poem "The Four Quartets," "the end of all our exploring/Will be to arrive where we started/

And know the place for the first time."[1] Trusting and following this calling to its ultimate denouement, spiritual awakening, rather than relying on some preestablished agenda or path, is a distinguishing characteristic of the pathless path. In the end, you are the path—the pathless path is unique to you.

My Own Journey on the Pathless Path

My own journey on the pathless path began with the loss of my mother at the tender age of fifteen and drew me first through the writers of the Beat generation to what at the time was the enigmatic and little-known practice of Zen. After years of reading the few books available on the subject back in the early sixties and minoring in Asian studies in college, I ended up in a zendo in New York City in the spring of 1969. The incense, the ritual, the bowing, the silence, all felt somehow familiar and resonant, as if I recognized them from a previous life. The talk for the evening was given by a woman my mother's age who said, in a soft and reassuring voice, that zazen (Zen meditation) was a way to bring you to your long-lost home. As a young man cut adrift by the loss of my mother, homecoming was exactly what I was seeking. I became a born-again Zen student and ordained as a monk five years later.

Fortunately, I had a series of teachers who counseled an alternative approach to the traditional and largely formalistic Zen taught in the monasteries of Japan. My first teacher, something of a renegade who had left the traditional role of temple priest to teach in the West, advised the practice of guerilla Zen—that is, the Zen of everyday life outside traditional forms—and admonished me to never call myself a Buddhist. A poet and master calligrapher, he embodied the true Zen spirit of spontaneous and idiosyncratic expression. The natural world also became a powerful teacher, as I found myself inspired by the eccentric mountain recluses and poets of Tang dynasty China for whom the mountains were the body of the Buddha and the rivers his tongue. In the spirit of direct transmission outside the scriptures recommended by the founder of Zen in China, I didn't read much Buddhist philosophy but preferred to find my guidance in the practice of meditation.

Eventually I spent some time in more structured Zen settings, but in the end I felt it was too restrictive and dry and set off on a more intuitive journey, informed by my many years of intensive meditation and guided only by what felt right and true for me. I sampled men's retreats and archetypal astrology, studied Jungian psychology and Gestalt therapy, practiced Tibetan Dzogchen-Mahamudra and a little Vipassana, and eventually stumbled on another unconventional teacher, a Western master of Advaita Vedanta, who taught what he called the "direct approach" to truth. Don't make meditation a habit, he advised, only use it as a laboratory to discover the meditator. Under his guidance I finally returned to my true home and took up my headquarters there. Through all this meandering I trusted that the different traditions all led to the same realization because, I believed, there's only one essential truth but many pointers home.

When I look back, I can see the hidden wisdom in the path my seeking took as I followed my inner guidance, though at the time I only knew what my heart and intuition were telling me and trusted it. Rather than dabbling like a dilettante or trying to figure out which way to go by comparing and contrasting different approaches but never really diving in, I threw myself wholeheartedly into each approach, learned what I needed to learn, and moved on when I felt complete. In particular, I was drawn to teachers who seemed to genuinely embody and transmit the awakened understanding they taught—and left those I ultimately discovered did not.

Of course, everyone has their own version of the pathless path; mine is just one potentially helpful example. The most important thing is that you develop and trust your inner guidance system and discover the path that has heart for you. Fortunately, there are many more good teachers available these days than back when I was meandering, most of them steeped in, or born into, Western culture and language, and you can find excellent teachings to choose from online without leaving home. (For the value and pitfalls of teachers, see chapter 5.) Once you're clear on which teachers and teachings appeal to you most, you have an opportunity to give them your wholehearted attention and energetic involvement and see where they take you. (For more on wholeheartedness and the other qualities that conduce to awakening, see chapter 3.)

The Direct Approach and the Pathless Path

The notion of the "pathless path" lies at the heart of the direct approach to spiritual awakening that I offer in my books, retreats, and programs. Essentially, the approach provides verbal pointers, guided meditations, self-inquiry exercises, and other skillful means that invite you to wake up directly to your natural state of nondual presence and essential inseparability from Being itself. More progressive and prescriptive approaches to truth may certainly play a part in your pathless path, as long as you don't take to heart their counsel that you need to achieve something new or cultivate qualities you don't already have. (For a detailed discussion on direct and progressive approaches, see chapter 4.) Remember, you already are what you're seeking, you just need to learn to recognize it and abide there.

Beyond even the direct approach, and perhaps the most pathless of paths, is to simply recognize that this luminous, sacred, and indivisible reality right now is what you are essentially—and just be it. No path is necessary to take you there. But only the maturest of souls can even understand what this directive means, let alone follow it, so the direct approach offers an actual path constructed of steps and stages that end up leading, paradoxically, to where you already are.

After many years of teaching the direct approach in the School for Awakening, which I've offered every year since 2007, I thought it best to condense the teachings into a book while they're still fresh in my mind and make them accessible to a wider audience. Over the years, hundreds of people have passed through the School, and a significant number have experienced some measure of awakening to their essential spiritual nature.

Of course, the School is not just a collection of pointers and practices, it's a living and lived experience with a group of kindred spirits and the live presence of a teacher. But I hope this book offers a glimpse of what others have learned there.

About This Book

Unlike many books on spiritual awakening, this one is not only or even primarily a collection of pointers and practices, though it does include an abundance of both. Rather, it's more of a road map to the pathless path itself, a guidebook to what can't be charted or anticipated, an overview of where the journey may take you and how to deal with the challenges and breakthroughs you encounter along the way. The book offers recommendations from my experience as seeker and teacher on understanding the nature and trajectory of awakening, choosing the right teacher, navigating the direct approach, working with challenging emotions and mind-states, engaging in awakened relationships, and appreciating the effect of past trauma on the path. Experiment with the experiential offerings and let yourself gravitate to the teachings and pointers that resonate for you. And be sure to take your time, especially if you're new to this approach—nondual wisdom offers a radically different perspective on life that must be contemplated slowly and repeatedly, and digested and assimilated gradually, until it takes hold and transforms you from the inside

The Meaning of Nondual Wisdom

Nondual wisdom involves the direct experiential knowing that subject and object, inside and outside, self and other, are in essence not two (nondual) and inseparable, though they may appear to be distinct and separate at the everyday level. Only the One exists—Being, consciousness, God, spirit, the nondual field—expressing itself in a multitude of forms. Not surprisingly, this truth is inherently paradoxical and not readily understood by the conceptual mind that prefers clear-cut distinctions and polarities—black or white, this or that, me or you. The nondual nature of reality needs to be apperceived, in a moment out of time and beyond the limitations of conceptual thought, in a unitive experience variously known as spiritual awakening, *kensho* (Japanese), *prajna* (Sanskrit), or *gnosis* (Greek). In the absence of such a transformative experience, the perennial philosophy is just another collection of concepts that has no power to transform our lives in beneficial ways but can be useful in pointing the way to the direct recognition on which it's based.

A Note on the Title

My working title for this book was "Endless Awakening" because, as I explain in the final chapter, my own experience and work with students has revealed to me over the years that spiritual awakening comes in as many shapes and sizes as there are people to awaken, and that the process of awakening takes a lifetime and at the same time is constantly fresh and new. Alas, the title had already been used in recent years by another book in a similar field, as had my second favorite, "Boundless Awakening." My editors at Shambhala then chose "Infinite Awakening," which they found "expansive, open-ended, aspirational, and evocative," much like the original was intended to be. At first, I had concerns that this new title might seem a bit presumptuous and offer more than the book could deliver. But after some discussion I agreed that yes, our natural state of awakened awareness has no limits or boundaries, and the pathless path does indeed invite us to awaken infinitely in every direction. In this spirit I invite you to enjoy your own infinite and endless awakening, with this book as your guide.

1

What Does Spiritual Awakening Really Mean?

Genuine spiritual awakening—at least of the nondual variety—is the recognition, in a moment out of time, that the way we've been perceiving reality has been mistaken and inside out. Despite the conventional or consensus view we've been conditioned to believe is true, there is no separate subject or self localized in here (the body) that's perceiving a reality out there (beyond the body). There is only one nondual reality—boundless, luminous, undivided, and all-pervasive—which is empty of substantiality and awake to itself.

This recognition isn't inherently complex. In fact, once you see it and fully take it in, it feels natural—even obvious. But when you first glimpse it, it often creates an upheaval in the mind—a fundamental shift in your sense of identity that can feel disorienting or even unsettling. After all, it cuts through the familiar illusion of solidity, separation, and the duality of subject and object on which our conventional worldview is based. In the words of the great twentieth-century sage Sri Nisargadatta Maharaj, "I am That."[1] Inside and outside are not two.

This realization can never belong to a someone, because as soon as we try to hold on to it and identify with it, we constellate a separate self and find ourselves outside it again. All the teachings and pointers come down to this simple truth, though the words and subtle distinctions may differ. What makes this truth elusive and difficult to recognize are all the many ways the mind resists and obscures it. Without the mind's conditioning and confusion, awakening would be so clear and unarguable that we would not need a path to it at all. Instead, we glimpse it, lose sight of it, misunderstand it, forget it, make an identity of it, discount it, overthink it, objectify it, fixate on it, and often ignore it completely. The recognition, and the nature of reality it recognizes, are simple; the human mind and heart are infinitely complex.

This book is a testament to our complexity. In our search for this recognition, which is our natural condition, nearer to us than breath itself, we constellate a path or journey to achieve it, which of course presents its own pitfalls and problems, distancing us from the very thing we already are. Hence the term "pathless path"—there's no place to go, yet a path keeps appearing before us. Not that we have a choice to do anything other than follow it, because we inevitably bring a lifetime of conditioning to each moment that obscures the truth and doesn't fall away in a heartbeat. Once we awaken, we're invited to investigate this conditioning and gradually release its hold over us, though it may take a lifetime.

In reality, most awakenings do not happen as neatly and succinctly as the one I just described. Often an awakening occurs as a kind of download of nondual wisdom that reveals itself gradually—like a zip file that you have to click on to reveal what's inside. Initially the emphasis may be on one or another aspect of the multifaceted jewel of reality that we awaken to. For example, we may see through the apparent solidity into the inherent insubstantiality or emptiness of manifest reality. We may fall out of the separate self into a deeper ground of silence and stillness beneath all the noise and activity. We may be overtaken by an experience of the oneness or inseparability of all phenomena. We may be flooded by feelings of unconditional love and joy without source or cause. Or we may transcend the limited perspective of the separate self and open into the vast expanse of awake awareness that includes this manifest reality in its embrace—and is ultimately seen to be inseparable from it.

Where these different forms and flavors of awakening align is that they all involve a kind of figure-ground shift in the locus of our identity from the separate self in here, apparently gazing out at a world out there, to the recognition that the so-called separate self is just another arising in the boundaryless openness/silence/stillness/oneness that we actually are. Once this is seen, it becomes impossible to completely unsee it and subscribe to the outmoded worldview we've so suddenly been forced to relinquish, and we may spend the rest of our lives coming to terms with, assimilating, and ultimately embodying the profound and ineffable truth we've discovered.

Pointer: Always Already Awake

Even though awakening is often experienced as a powerful breakthrough that transforms your worldview and way of being in the world, it's actually a recognition of the way things have always been, the nondual reality that is always already the case. As a result, it's not an altered state, but a return to your natural state of inherent wakefulness and wisdom. No effort is required to realize the ever-present Self, says the Advaita sage Ramana Maharshi. Realization is already there—you just need to let go of illusion.

A Radical Turnaround in Consciousness

"Awakening" is the term we use to describe this shift because it involves a radical change of perspective similar to the one we experience when we rise up out of sleep into the light of everyday life. Ordinary, consensus reality is like a dream with an imaginary me at the center that obscures our clear seeing of the deeper nature of reality just as it is, however that deeper reality may be expressed and understood. When we wake up, the metaphor goes, we step out of the dream narrative we've inhabited into the light of a new life of freedom, peace, and love.

Spiritual awakenings have occurred since time immemorial, no doubt as long as human beings have been roaming the planet and exploring their inner life. The Upanishads, Indian texts that date back more than three thousand years and form the basis of the Hindu teachings known as Vedanta, speak of awakening to our divine essence, our eternal Self (*atman*), which is identical with and inseparable from God itself. More than twenty-five hundred years ago the Buddha, an Indian prince whose name means "awakened one," guided his followers to use self-reflection and introspection (known as meditation) to awaken to the profound truth that there is indeed no self (anatman) but only reality endlessly unfolding. (Exactly what the Buddha said is impossible to know, since his teachings were written down only five hundred years after his death, and hundreds of schools have grown up in the millennia since he lived, based on the profound realizations of his disciples and descendants.)

The Buddhist tradition, and its Hindu cousin Advaita Vedanta (the nondual current within the Vedanta tradition), are founded on the primary importance of this radical metanoia, or turnaround in consciousness. The story of the Buddha, who renounced a life of pleasure and luxury to seek lasting release from suffering after witnessing sickness, old age, and death, is an archetypal quest with universal resonance that's been inspiring seekers throughout the world for thousands of years. Tibetan teaching stories, Zen koans, and the biographies of saints and sages in India and throughout the world are full of moments of sudden illumination—when the pebble strikes bamboo or the master speaks in paradoxical ways—that have confounded and motivated sincere seekers to find their own way.

In the modern era everyone on the pathless path knows the story of Venkataraman, the sixteen-year-old South Indian boy who suddenly felt himself taken by an impulse to discover what death was really like and thirty minutes later awakened to his deathless spiritual nature. Shortly thereafter he settled beneath a sacred mountain devoted to Shiva, the Hindu god who embodies awakened consciousness, and spent the next sixty years teaching there as the sage Ramana Maharshi.

In Buddhism this radical turnaround in consciousness is known as *ashraya paravritti*, which literally means a transformation in the basis or foundation of consciousness, a profound upheaval and reconfiguration of our way of perceiving reality, in which we shift from conceptual knowing based on our conditioning to direct, clear seeing of the way it actually is. Throughout the history of Mahayana Buddhism, of which the Zen and Tibetan traditions have been principal examples, this transformative turnaround has been considered the point and purpose of study and practice, whether through progressive skillful means or direct pointing.

In the Zen tradition, which I practiced for many years as a monk, this turnaround in consciousness—known as *kensho* (seeing true nature) or *satori* (enlightenment)—is precipitated by "taking the backward step to turn the light inward to illuminate the Self," in the words of Eihei Dogen, one of the founders of Japanese Zen. Most of the time our awareness is focused outward on objects, but meditation and self-inquiry turn awareness inward and back upon itself to discover that pure awareness is what we are fundamentally.

Buddhism and Vedanta may be unique in the value they place on awakening, but most of the world's spiritual traditions acknowledge an awakening of some kind, a rebirth out of the old way of being into a new life or dispensation, a conversion or metanoia, a deep recognition of the divine spark or eternal soul that lies beneath our external manifestation. In the words of Jesus (John 3:3), "Unless one is born again, one cannot see the kingdom of God"—that is, the sacred, nondual dimension of being.

The apostle Paul, who had his own radical awakening on the road to Damascus, says in 1 Corinthians 13:12, "For now we see through a glass, darkly; but then face to face: now I know in part; but then shall

I know even as also I am known." In these words, he appears to be describing the moment of meeting the divine directly and realizing that seer and seen, subject and object, are not two, but are nondual. Meister Eckhart points to the same recognition in his famous dictum "The eye with which I see God is the eye with which God sees me"—that is, the seeker is the sought, the looker what he or she is looking for.[2] In early Christianity and the Western hermetic tradition this nondual knowing is called *gnosis* (the root of the English word "know"), which, like the Sanskrit term *jnana* and the Buddhist *prajna* (all three derived from the same Indo-European root as the word "know"), means direct apperception not mediated by the conceptual mind.

The Truth or Reality to Which We Awaken

Although it can be difficult to describe in words, the nondual insight or perspective we awaken to is quite simple. There is only this one, undivided reality, which is always only here and now. This reality is beyond categories of time and space and includes all manifestation in its boundaryless embrace, yet it is essentially luminous, empty of substantiality, and inherently awake to itself. For those who have realized it for themselves, it can be encapsulated in the words "I am That." Of course, this definition is merely a pointer to what must be directly apperceived to be understood.

Simple though it may be, this truth is so radically different from our accustomed perspective that awakening to it is often accompanied by a variety of spiritual states or experiences, like bliss, rapture, kundalini energy, absorption in an object of veneration, beatific visions, awe, devotion, or a feeling of merging with all things. These states may arise before, during, and after the awakening and are often confused with genuine awakening; indeed, some people mistakenly make them the goal of their search.

But states come and go, constantly morph and change, and inevitably elude our attempts to hold on to or recreate them. By contrast, awakened awareness abides as the eternal background of all states, the ultimate experiencer, which does not come or go and can't be objectified in any way. When we awaken, we recognize that we are this background (or home ground) of awakened awareness—pure subjectivity in which all experience arises and passes away. States occur to someone; awakening is the recognition that the separate someone to whom these states apparently occur doesn't really exist. States are just dreams of various kinds from which we will eventually awaken. Awakened awareness is the eternal nonstate beneath and behind all dreams, the blank screen on which all states are projected and into which they eventually dissolve, like waves returning to the boundless ocean.

In the world's spiritual traditions, including the esoteric current in just about every religion, this nondual reality is given a variety of different names. In theistic traditions, it's called "God," which makes it difficult to recognize as our true identity and natural state because there's usually a proscription against identifying oneself with the divine. In Hinduism it's *atman-Brahman*, the divine inner-outer dual unity; *satchitananda* (being-consciousness-bliss); or *Shiva-Shakti* in the tantric traditions like Kashmir Shaivism. In Advaita it's called simply "consciousness," and in Zen it's "buddha nature" (*tathagatagarbha*) or "true self," though various masters in koans down through the ages have called it a variety of things, including "shit stick," "one bright pearl," and "the cypress tree in the garden." In Tibetan Dzogchen it's known as *rigpa*.

Many sages have described it as a luminous sphere that contains all of reality within its boundless embrace; a bright jewel or pearl beyond price; a drop of dew, glimmering in the light, that contains the whole universe but lasts just an instant and is gone in a heartbeat. For the Greek philosopher Empedocles, it's the circle whose center is everywhere and circumference is nowhere. In the Tibetan Buddhist tradition it's the wish-fulfilling jewel, and in the Gospels Jesus likens the kingdom of heaven (understood in the esoteric tradition as spiritual illumination) to a pearl of great price worth sacrificing all earthly treasures to obtain.

However it's experienced, what we awaken to is a precious recognition or deep inner knowing that's indestructible, though it may fade into the background and wax and wane in clarity. The source and wellspring of all love, peace, joy, wisdom, compassion, and fulfillment, it both belongs to us, as our true Self, and is beyond any self or belonging, the sacred nature of reality itself revealing itself through this particular body and mind. According to the sage Ramana Maharshi, it's expressed most succinctly in the Bible when God says to Moses: I am that I am.

Pointer: No One Has Ever Been Awakened

The paradox and irony of the awakening journey is that you can never claim the achievement for yourself because what you've achieved is the realization that the separate self you supposed yourself to be has never existed. For the ego that strives to realize and attain something substantial for itself, it's a fruitless search. With spiritual teachers as well, beware those who claim to be enlightened, because true awakening inevitably includes the humorous and humbling recognition that there's no one who can possibly own that illustrious and elusive adjective. No wonder the Zen monks in the koans end up laughing at the irony when they experience satori!

The Impact of Awakening

Because awakening is often a powerful experience that occurs suddenly without anticipation and lands in the midst of the ordinary mind like a meteor from another realm, beyond space and time, it may have a dramatic and lasting impact and leave a series of profound changes in its wake, both beneficent and challenging. Our accustomed dualistic worldview has been shattered, or at least momentarily turned inside out, and just as an earthquake may cause buildings to fall, an awakening may leave cherished beliefs and concepts shattered in its wake. How we respond to this upheaval depends largely on the power and depth of the awakening, our particular psychology, and the preparation we've undergone to get to this point.

The limited worldview or dream we've inhabited for a lifetime has fallen away, and with it the sense of limitation and constriction it has imposed. Now we realize that we're the boundless space in which experience unfolds, not the contents of experience, and we may even have the sense that the mind and body we've taken ourselves to be has dropped off. The illusion of separation has dropped as well, and we may experience a profound intimacy with our surroundings and the people we encounter. Many people respond to this moment with feelings of joy, rapture, laughter, and/or profound peace. In the old Zen stories the classic response is uproarious laughter at the realization that what you're experiencing now is what you've always been.

But for people whose identification with their mind is still so strong, often because they haven't spent time in meditation opening up space between awareness and the contents of awareness, the experience may be met with terror as the mind realizes that the rug has been pulled out from under it and there's no longer an accustomed ground of beliefs, concepts, and identities to catch its fall. For those who were abused or abandoned as children, this groundlessness may even evoke the fear of annihilation they experienced when their survival was threatened at such a young age and create an ambivalence about awakening itself. For example, the ambivalence may take the form of at once seeking to deepen the awakening because it offers the possibility of greater freedom from suffering but at the same time avoiding it because it evokes so much fear. (For more on trauma and awakening, see chapter 9.)

In the remainder of this book we'll be exploring the long-term impact and ramifications of awakening and the lifelong journey of deepening, clarifying, and living from it. In the short term, here are some of the mind-states and reactions you may encounter in the wake of awakening. They may last for a few minutes, a few hours, or weeks and months, and in rare cases may become your abiding experience. (Some of these are discussed at length in my book *Wake Up Now.*) If any of these reactions make everyday life difficult, you may want to consult a therapist who specializes in spiritual emergence.

Pleasant

Sense of being the boundless and boundaryless space in which life is unfolding

Freedom from identification with thoughts and feelings

Loss of any identity whatsoever and the inability to find a separate someone inside

Laughter at the emptiness and insubstantiality (dreamlike nature) of it all

Deep peace and equanimity accompanied by an absence of past reactivity

Spontaneous upwelling of feelings of gratitude, appreciation, reverence, and love

Pleasurable, nourishing mind-states like bliss, rapture, ecstasy, mild kundalini

Unpleasant

Frightening groundlessness and loss of boundaries

Fear of annihilation

Unexpected resurfacing of repressed memories and difficult, painful feelings from the past

Momentary disorientation, derealization, depersonalization

Oscillation between rapture and terror

Powerful, disruptive kundalini

Neither pleasant nor unpleasant

Alternating between getting and losing the awakening

Trying to suppress or ignore the awakening

Becoming inflated with the illusion that one is now an "enlightened person" (an oxymoron)

Becoming detached and aloof from a world of people and objects that's now been seen as empty or illusory

Is Awakening Sudden, Gradual—or Optional?

In Asian spirituality this transformative turnaround in consciousness, this metanoia or satori, has traditionally been considered the goal and fruition of the spiritual path. Die before you die, enjoin the Zen masters. Realize the nature of mind, encourage the Tibetan tulkus and rinpoches. Allow the illusion of the separate self to dissolve in the ocean of consciousness, teach the Advaita sages. Even Jesus, who may have been influenced by the Upanishads, encouraged people to die and be reborn.[3]

But different traditions differ on how they believe this awakening occurs. Is it a sudden and instantaneous realization in which the separate self, with all its suffering, confusion, and reactivity, falls away completely, leaving no trace? Or is it a gradual process of recognition and refinement that unfolds over many years of practice and insight? This distinction has been debated and argued for thousands of years in both Hinduism and Buddhism. In the Chan (Zen) tradition in China, the sudden and gradual schools, in the north and south respectively, debated for centuries and finally agreed to disagree and reconciled their differences with the recognition that it was both: a sudden breakthrough followed by a lifetime of deepening and refinement. This is essentially the perspective I offer in this book and teach in the School for Awakening. The initial breakthrough is the first (and most important) step on the journey of awakening, with more breakthroughs to come as awakening unfolds.

Some people do have a powerful, knock-your-socks-off breakthrough experience that reveals the truth of their nondual spiritual nature once and for all. Many others glimpse it little by little, in short bursts of insight, until the final moment when all doubt falls away and seeking comes to an end. Not surprisingly, given our diversity as a species, awakening reveals itself in very different ways for different people, and the natural trajectory of awakening passes through many stages and dimensions. Either way, we first need to cross the threshold, experience the turnaround for ourselves, and realize the nondual truth directly. (For a detailed description of the stages and dimensions of awakening, see chapter 2.)

These days, unfortunately, there are many teachers of awakening in the West who seem to question the need for awakening entirely. From this perspective, popularly known as neo-Advaita (or what I call "awakening lite"), you're already awakened, there's nothing new to see or achieve, everything is perfect as it is, and you merely need to"call off the search and be who you are," in the words of a popular pointer, without any effort, practice, or inquiry on your part. In fact, effort is considered counterproductive because there's no doer, no separate someone to do anything, and any doing just takes you away from what you always already are and reifies the illusion of a separate self struggling to stay in control.

The teaching that you are already awake is essentially accurate; the problem is that calling off the search before you've found what you're looking for—the inherent wakefulness that the great masters point to—is like sitting down in the midst of preparing a meal and pretending you're no longer hungry. Not until you've cooked the food and eaten your fill can you genuinely claim that you're done. As the Zen tradition puts it, painted cakes can't satisfy your hunger—just as comforting nondual platitudes can't give you the deep insight and the turnaround in consciousness that you so understandably crave.

In Zen, this paradox is known as the gateless gate. Once you realize the truth, you discover that the barrier or gate that seemed to separate you from it was just an illusion—there never was a barrier after all. But until you've passed through the gate and realized this truth for yourself, it gives you no lasting relief. The teaching that you're already enlightened can function as a skillful means designed to wake you up; as a platitude, it's no more than a soothing collection of concepts that divert your attention from the awakening that you ultimately seek.

Awakening lite appeals to our need-to-have-it-all-now, instant gratification culture, where young people with minimal skills become social-media influencers and journalists take time-honored concepts, water them down for easy consumption, and produce *New York Times* bestsellers. Genuine, life-transforming awakening requires devotion, motivation, intention, and above all wholehearted investigation and practice, qualities I'll talk about at length in chapter 3.

In my many years of experience as a teacher of awakening, I've found that most people on the path aren't satisfied until they experience the truth of their being fully and decisively, in all its clarity and power. They're seeking a complete and undeniable recognition that transforms their claustrophobic, egocentric worldview once and for all. Otherwise, they're neither here nor there, not fully mired in the old illusion yet not fully awake either, and they continue to doubt the validity of the reality they've glimpsed. This is why Zen masters and Dzogchen teachers keep testing their students to make sure their awakening is complete and fully realized. Otherwise, the new and transformed life we aspire to can't come into being and we can't legitimately claim awakening as our birthright or causeless happiness as our natural state.

Reflect and Inquire

If you're new to the journey of spiritual awakening, take some time to reflect on the teachings and pointers in this chapter. Do they make intuitive sense? Have you had glimpses or glimmers of the undivided, nondual nature of reality they describe? Or does awakening seem foreign but somehow appealing? Do you feel drawn to the shift in identity that awakening entails, or are you quite content with the identity you currently have?

If you are familiar with these teachings or have experienced some awakening yourself, notice how you respond to the discussion about the radical and life-transforming nature of genuine awakening. What feelings and concerns does it evoke? How do you imagine awakening would change your life? What are your ideas, preconceptions, and expectations about awakening that might get in the way of recognizing it when it occurs?

Q&A

The following section provides answers to frequently asked questions to help clarify and expand on the chapter's key points.

Q: You describe genuine awakening as involving a radical turnaround in consciousness with a profound and lasting impact. I've had what I would consider an awakening, but it wasn't as dramatic or complete as the one you describe. Now I seem to have lost it, or at least it's receded into the background, and I can't find it. Was it genuine? What should I do now?

A: Don't worry about the drama, it's unnecessary and often no more than a distraction. Remember, awakening comes in many shapes, sizes, durations, and levels of clarity and depth. The mark of a true awakening is that you recognize that you're not the contents of your experience, you're the one who experiences but can't itself become an experience. The recognition may recede into the background, but it will continue to inform your experience of life going forward in subtle and not-so-subtle ways. Self-inquiry or the contemplation of pointers may help nudge it to the foreground. In the end, what you've discovered is what you essentially are, so it can't go anywhere, only your connection with it may seem to wax and wane. Treasure and nurture this recognition like a seed, and it will eventually blossom into full nondual realization.

Q: If I experience the fear of annihilation when I glimpse the emptiness and groundlessness of all phenomena, what can I do about it? I must admit I'm afraid of the fear.

A: Just let it arise and pass away without struggling with it or trying to get rid of it. Fear is just another experience that comes and goes, and you are the experiencer that abides, free of any experience. Eventually the mind adjusts and gets used to the groundlessness, especially as you awaken to your abiding spiritual nature as the experiencer. If the fear continues to disturb you, even as your realization deepens and unfolds, it may be an indication that psychological issues have been triggered and you may benefit from consulting with a therapist familiar with meditation and spiritual awakening.[4]

Meditation: Who Am I?

As human beings, we use the term "I" repeatedly, as if we know what it means. I see, I think, I feel, I taste, I touch, I want. But who or what or where is this I? You give it ultimate power and value in your life. You go to great lengths to fulfill its needs and defend it against attack. But do you really know what it is?

The cells in your body have died and been replaced multiple times over a lifetime. Your body bears little resemblance to the body you had when you were five or ten or twenty. Your thoughts, your feelings, are totally fresh, totally new. Your inner narrative is changing constantly. Yet you use the very same word "I" that you used as a child, as if you know intuitively that what it refers to has remained unchanged over the years.

Where is this abiding, unchanging I? Anything you can experience is an object of your awareness. When you say, "I see a tree, I hear a bird, I know a fact," the tree, the bird, the fact is an object and I is the subject. For this reason, you can never know or experience the I. Because as soon as you think you've grasped it and turn it into an object, it eludes your grasp.

This meditation leads you in a time-honored form of self-inquiry that has the potential to reveal the true nature of this abiding, unchanging I, the ultimate subject of all objects.

Rest your awareness on the sensations of the coming and going of your breath. Now open your awareness to the sounds around you, the traffic, the birds, the voices in the background. Clearly, sounds are being heard, but who or what is hearing? If you say, "I am, I'm the one who's hearing," ask yourself, who is this I and where is it located?

Open your eyes and allow your awareness to settle on a particular object like a table, a chair, a bookcase, a desk. As you gaze at this object, ask yourself, who is seeing? Clearly the object is seen, but who or what is seeing? Again, you may say, "I am, of course," but who is this I and where is it located?

Set aside any conceptual answers. For example, ideas like "I'm awareness" or "I'm a being of light" won't provide the answer you seek. Just relax, breathe softly, and let your inquiry be direct and experiential. Who am I? Who am I really?

Like many people, you may believe that you're your brain or your thoughts. But both of these, the brain and the thoughts, can be experienced. You can sense your brain, think your thoughts. The deeper question is, who is sensing, who is thinking?

If your inquiry becomes too effortful, too mental, just relax and sit quietly again. After a few moments, you can begin questioning, but not as an intellectual exercise. Let it be a whole-body search for the ultimate experiencer. See if you can find it. Instead of who am I or what am I, you might prefer asking, who is thinking this thought, who is feeling this feeling, who is seeing through these eyes right now? Or you can ask, to whom is this thought, this feeling, this visual image, this moment occurring?

The point of all these questions is not to engage the mind, because the mind inevitably gnaws on questions endlessly, like a dog on a bone. Instead, just drop the question into the stillness of your being, like a pebble that you might drop into a forest pool.

Spend as long as you like on this inquiry, and when you feel complete, just set it aside and go about your day.

2

The Stages of Awakening

Spiritual awakening is a radical shift in the locus of our identity, a sudden transformation in consciousness that occurs in a moment out of time and turns our accustomed reality inside out and upside down. Sometimes it happens spontaneously and without preparation or expectation, even to those who have no spiritual interest or inclinations. More often, we stumble upon it after a series of glimmers, upwellings, intimations, or glimpses of a deeper, more luminous or sacred dimension of reality that gives sparkle, divinity, or meaning to our everyday lives but is not yet clearly recognized or understood. Walking in the forest, we drop into a timeless silence beneath all the birdsong. Making love with our partner, we lose all sense of separation and merge with our surroundings. Sitting in meditation, we experience in our own heart the love and light at the heart of reality.

Before, we took ourselves to be a separate self located inside the body-mind and surrounded by a world of separate objects with which we interact and that affect, threaten, benefit, or impinge upon us. After awakening, we realize that we are the awareness in which reality unfolds, and at the deepest level we're not separate from this seemingly external world of objects that we're aware of.

These glimpses and glimmers may draw us inexorably toward awakening like the proverbial moth to the flame of truth. At the same time, suffering may drive us toward it, as we seek to free ourselves from the dream of a limited, painful, claustrophobic reality in which we're enthralled. As a result, we may practice meditation, seek out a teacher and receive teachings, and set out on the pathless path, hoping to return to our long-lost home like the prodigal child who's lost their way. In the iconic oxherding pictures of Zen,[1] the early stages—finding the footprints and catching a glimpse of the ox—refer to discovering that awakening is actually a possibility and that a path exists in the underbrush to lead us toward it.

Whether it's spontaneous and unexpected or precipitated by practice, the journey of awakening, once it begins, tends to follow a certain trajectory. The unfolding is not usually linear but generally meanders in more of a spiral, crisscrossing similar terrain repeatedly as it reveals itself, and not necessarily proceeding in the same order. We may have glimpses of a deeper level that inspire us but don't become entirely clear, and we may keep getting stuck in the same place again and again. In some cases the initial awakening may involve a download of wisdom that includes all subsequent stages in it, a kind of zip file that may take months or years to unpack.

In the end, everyone's journey is unique, and there is no cookie-cutter trajectory. But at least five stages do seem to keep presenting themselves. I offer them not as a standard against which to judge your progress, but as a template to help you locate your experience along the arc when you feel lost or confused. (For a reminder of what awakening is, what we awaken to, and the initial impact of awakening and our reaction to it, see chapter 1.)

Disidentification from the Contents of Awareness

Most of us, most of the time, identify with our thoughts and feelings and take ourselves to be the story of our lives, the personal history with a "me" at the center. Because we're totally attached or Velcroed to this story, with its plans for the future, anxieties about the present, and regrets about the past, we live in a claustrophobic inner world with little or no space free of concerns to breathe, step back, and simply be. The narrative is who we believe ourselves to be, where we begin and end, and the drama seems quite solid, real, and consequential. (For more on the narrative or dream we inhabit, see chapter 6.)

Once you start to reflect, meditate, or inquire, however, you recognize that this narrative is merely content arising in awareness and not necessarily the truth about who you are. As the one who meditates or inquires, you realize, I'm located here, wherever that is, and the contents—the thoughts, feelings, memories, beliefs—are there, separate from me. The whole process appears to be taking place in the mind, and awareness begins to crystallize out from the contents of which it's aware.

Before, I was completely identified with the thoughts and feelings, the fears, beliefs, jealousies, and resentments; now I realize that I'm the one sitting here being aware of them. I don't exactly know yet who this one is, but I understand that whoever it is, it's not identical with what it's aware of. This insight often dawns after a first meditation retreat or weeks or months of meditating regularly on your own.

What are the implications of this realization? What does it mean? Who am I really? You haven't begun to answer these crucial questions yet, but at least your identification with the contents of mind has begun to loosen. Though it may come quite early in the process, this insight is generally the first step in the trajectory of awakening and can be quite powerful when it finally dawns.

Often people stay here for an extended period, hanging out on the threshold but not quite stepping over, knowing they're not the content yet not quite knowing what the context really is. Meditators who find that their practice gives them the relative ease of being and freedom from stress, anxiety, and depression they originally came to it for may be hesitant to delve deeper. After all, crossing the threshold may upset the equilibrium they've worked so hard to achieve and precipitate a momentous shift in which the familiar identification with an observing ego drops away to reveal their true nature as awakened awareness.

Pointer: Awakening Is a Gift

I describe the process of awakening in great detail in this chapter not so you can make it happen according to some preestablished schedule or agenda, which you definitely can't, but rather as a guide for when it begins to happen to you, as it always does, spontaneously, unpredictably, and free of any control on your part. Awakening to truth is a gift, catalyzed by your motivation, aspiration, and sincerity and orchestrated and delivered by truth alone.

Realizing Oneself as Awareness Itself

If you continue to meditate, reflect, and inquire, you soon stumble upon the recognition that the one who is aware of the content of your life is itself not more content, but context only, awake awareness free of any localization or objectivity. Even the meditator you've recognized as separate from the contents of meditation has itself been localized and objectified, and you realize that awareness itself is pure subjectivity that can't be objectified in any way. The observer seemingly located in the body-mind is just more content in awareness, and I am this awareness, free of all contents and any localization in space and time. I am the awake, aware space in which the narrative I take myself to be arises and passes away. I am the ultimate subject of all objects.

For most people this is the transformative moment of true awakening, the significant shift that jolts you out of the dream and signals the transition from sleep to wakefulness. From now on you can't fully identify with the drama of your life; you've moved beyond it and know yourself to be essentially free of it. Even though you may get seduced back into believing it again, hopefully for shorter and shorter periods of time, you now know without doubt that it is in fact just a drama, and you're not one of the actors, you're the stage or screen on which the drama is projected and at the same time the one who is aware of it all, fundamentally untouched and undisturbed.

This powerful shift may be accompanied by a sense of disorientation, dislocation, disruption, upheaval, and fear of losing your ground or going crazy. After all, your accustomed identity, everything you thought you were, has revealed itself to be a dream. Now you know that you're awareness, free of identification, but you're probably not yet clear about the nature and parameters of this awareness. At this point you need to investigate this awareness and find out what it really is.

If you take the time necessary to explore this awareness through meditation or self-inquiry, you gradually discover that it has no limits or boundaries, it can't be objectified or located in space and time, and at the same time it includes all experience in its boundaryless embrace. You may recognize it as the deeper ground beneath all arising, the silence beneath all sound, the stillness beneath all activity, the sacred dimension that gives depth and meaning to life.

In traditions that emphasize transcendence rather than integrating awareness into everyday life, the realization that I am the ultimate subject, the pure witness outside space and time, the eternal Self free of all identification with the world of form, is regarded as the final resting place, the fruition of the search. There's nothing more to see. The pure witness is separate from the impure domain of manifestation, which is regarded as an illusion and the source of suffering, and the goal is to remain aloof and unsullied by the complications of life. There are currents in Theravada Buddhism, Indian Vedanta, and classical yoga philosophy that teach this view, and people who seriously dedicate themselves to this path generally renounce the world and practice in ashrams and monasteries, where their involvements are simplified and regulated. In Zen, on the other hand, getting stuck in emptiness and transcendence and failing to embrace the relative reality of everyday life is known as the Zen sickness to which some overzealous meditators may be prone.

But from the nondual perspective, this realization is incomplete and inherently dualistic and must complete itself in the recognition that subject and object, self and other, are not two. If I'm the witness, what about all those objects? Where do they fit in? And what is their relationship to this awareness that I know myself to be? This is the next phase or stage of realization. You may get glimpses of it early in the awakening process, but it may not be clear until later. You need to come down off your transcendent mountaintop and realize, in the words of the *Heart Sutra* chanted in Zen, that form is emptiness, and emptiness is form. The transcendent and immanent, essential and manifest, absolute and relative, are inextricably entwined and co-arising. Depending on your religious or philosophical orientation and the nature of your realization, this not-two can be understood and experienced in different ways: as God or spirit, consciousness, or buddha nature or true self. However you describe it, the apparent duality needs to dissolve in Being, the nondual field.

Pointer: Painted Cakes Can't Satisfy Your Hunger

Throughout the centuries the core insights and awakenings described in this chapter were closely guarded by the nondual wisdom traditions, in part because they might be misunderstood and misapplied, and in part because seekers might become fixated on the concepts and lose interest in discovering the deeper truth to which they point. Nowadays you can find these same once-secret teachings trumpeted widely on webinars, podcasts, and YouTube videos for listeners to do with them what they may—and, just as expected, many people can now parrot the teachings without having genuine experiences and insights of their own. But painted or pixelated cakes won't give you the satisfaction you crave, they're only signposts on an extended journey of self-realization. If the teachings you've encountered have whetted your appetite, now is the time to taste the real cakes directly for yourself.

Oneness of Awareness and Its Contents

Of course, you may awaken directly into the nondual and never need to pass through the stage of witness awareness. Both Zen and Tibetan Dzogchen-Mahamudra emphasize this direct recognition as the gate through which we enter when we experience satori (Zen) or recognize the nature of mind (Dzogchen). In one oft-quoted formulation from his treatise *Genjokoan*, Zen master Dogen puts it this way:

> To study the way of the Buddha is to study the self. To study the self is to forget the self. To forget the self is to be awakened by the ten thousand things. When awakened by the ten thousand things, your body and mind and the bodies and minds of others drop away. No trace of awakening remains, and this no-trace continues endlessly.[2]

Scholars and teachers have pored over these few sentences for hundreds of years in an attempt to understand their meaning with the conceptual mind, and devoted Zen students have contemplated them in zazen to precipitate an awakening. But what he's saying is not particularly arcane: True realization involves the dropping away of the illusion of separation and the recognition that inside and outside are undivided, not two—and even more, that the "stink of enlightenment," the mistaken sense that there is someone to get enlightened, falls away without a trace as well, and only reality, the nondual field, the eternal Now, abides. Again, form is no other than emptiness, and emptiness is no other than form.

The Mahamudra teaching poem "Tilopa's Song to Naropa" makes the same point just as succinctly:

> Gazing with sheer awareness
> into sheer awareness,
> habitual, abstract structures melt
> into the fruitful springtime of awakening.[3]

In other words, true awakening to the nature of mind involves recognizing that what is looking and what is looked at are not two, both are made up of pure awareness—and in this recognition the habitual conceptual structures of separation fall away, just as body and mind dropped away for Dogen.

My teacher Jean Klein, who taught Advaita but was strongly influenced by the nondual tantric tradition of Kashmir Shaivism, says it clearly as well: "When we consider the knower independently of the known, it reveals itself to be pure witness. When knowledge and the knower are [recognized to be] one, there is no longer a place for a witness."[4] Jean would often remind us that there is no separate perceiver and no separate object perceived, only perceiving, only experiencing, a dynamic process expressed by a verb rather than a concatenation of objects described by nouns. This realization resembles the one described by the historical Buddha, who taught that nothing is solid, substantial, permanent, or unchanging. Instead, existence consists of innumerable dharmas, discrete units of experience, endlessly arising and passing away in an ongoing stream of perception.

Despite these clear pointers, however, practitioners of all three traditions still tend to catch the Zen sickness and get stuck in the dualistic witness position. Here the pointers of the teacher can be crucial in nudging the student out of their limited view and into the complete recognition of nondual presence.

Only This, Only Now!

Even the stage of the oneness of subject and object involves a subtle duality in the form of a separate subject and object that then somehow merge into one. Beyond even oneness or no separation, there's only This, the nondual field, what Zen calls "suchness" or "thusness" and Advaita calls "consciousness," the endless no trace that Dogen describes. All trace of subject and object falls away, revealing the recognition that I never existed at all, there is only this one boundless reality, Being, consciousness, God, the one without a second, expressing itself in a myriad of forms. I'm not living this life as I suppose, life is living itself through me.

In the classic Zen formulation, this is the final stage of total ordinariness in which mountains are seen to be simply mountains again, and rivers to be just rivers. Nothing has ever been separate or apart from the nondual reality even for an instant, and the categories of sacred and profane no longer apply. Everything has only a single taste, the taste of Being. In the ten oxherding pictures, it's the ninth, returning to source. At the experiential level, everything is seen to be perfect and complete just as it is, no trace of self or enlightenment remains, and there's a constant, subtle joy or happiness without cause that permeates every experience.

For most people, having a glimpse of this ultimate nonduality, and perhaps even hanging out here for periods of time, is the final fruition of the awakening journey. As far as I can tell from my discussions with other nondual teachers, the falling away of any trace of a separate self and a complete merging with nondual reality—the final dissolution of the wave into the ocean of Being—is a rare occurrence in a living human being. Ramana Maharshi himself said that the identification with the body-mind is the final threshold that's not often crossed before the moment of physical death. Until then there may always be some level of identification, no matter how subtle, that ties us to this form and may kick in when our survival is at stake. Indeed, most of us would probably not want to go any further but would prefer to stay tethered to the human body in some way—especially since we don't live in an ashram or monastery or have someone to tend to our physical needs. (After his awakening at the age of sixteen, Ramana spent several years in complete surrender and ego-dissolution, unable to meet his own needs and taken care of by others. Eventually he emerged and began teaching, and an ashram was established around him.)

Awakened Embodiment and Transformation

Once we've fully and irrevocably realized that the nondual dimension of being—reality living itself without a separate someone in charge—is the true Self the masters describe, we may spend the rest of our lives aspiring to live as consistently as possible in alignment with this knowing. But the body-mind is inevitably imperfect and conditioned by life circumstances, and much of our meditation and self-inquiry post-awakening may be focused on revealing and releasing old patterns of identification and reactivity that prevent us from being an effective vehicle or vessel of this truth. As our awakening deepens and clarifies, we become more and more adept at recognizing what's not true, and is therefore the province of ego, and returning repeatedly to nondual presence, what I like to call awakened awareness.

At this point, these become the most important questions: How do I allow my life—my relationships, my work, my every moment—to become an expression of this deeper knowing? How do I drop the ego's ingrained resistance to what is and its addiction to control, and allow life to live through me without impediment? How can I recognize and step out of the dream my mind perpetuates and rest in clear seeing? How can I come to peace and happiness with the way things truly are? This is sometimes called "waking down": First we wake up out of the contents of our lives, then we wake out to include all of reality in the nondual field, and then we wake down into the seamless integration of the absolute and relative, sacred and ordinary, transcendent and immanent dimensions of life. This is the realm of the last oxherding picture, returning to the marketplace with helping hands, and it's the topic of the final chapters in this book.

Awakening Through the Body

Beyond these basic stages in the awakening process, I've found that awakening tends to mature and ripen down through the energy centers of the body, beginning in the upper chakras and gradually unfurling through the heart and into the belly center and root chakra. Again, everyone has their own unique trajectory, but there does appear to be some consistency to this unfolding.

By upper chakras I refer to the centers of subtle knowing and illumination located at the crown of the head and behind the forehead. (These are also centers associated with intellectual knowledge and conceptual thought.) Awakening here takes the form of expanded spaciousness and openness to experience as it is, the dropping away of identities and belief systems, greater freedom from narrative and self-image, and deep insight into the nature of reality. But awakening solely at this level may also be dry and detached, lack empathy and compassion, feel disconnected and abstract, and avoid engaging at the relational level. When people prefer to hang out here and avoid the psychological challenges of ordinary life, it's known as spiritual bypassing.

When awakening expands into the heart center, you shift from merely allowing your experience in an open and spacious way to welcoming and even embracing it just as it is without judgment. At the same time, you begin to feel a deep communion and compassion with all beings and a sense of no-separation at the intimate interrelational level. Boundaries around your heart drop away, you release accumulated anger and pain, the sense of separation with other people dissolves, and the oneness that may have felt abstract to you before now feels filled with warmth and love.

When the love and clarity of awakening move into the third chakra, at the level of the belly, you let go of your addiction to imposing your agenda on others and maintaining control of circumstances. You no longer feel you have to argue or defend your point of view. And when the second chakra in the lower abdomen awakens, deep emotional bonds and sexual connections lose their survival-level intensity and become more relaxed, open, affectionate, and playful.

When you awaken to the ground of being through the root chakra at the base of your spine, you experience a new level of trust in the unfolding at the existential level and a deep sense of surrender to the flow of life. "Not my will but thy will be done." Oneness now expresses itself through spontaneous and intuitive action for the benefit of the whole, and you know your body-mind to be merely a vehicle or portal through which life lives itself.

Of course, I've just described the ideal and uninterrupted embodiment of awakening down through the chakras, but it will inevitably be more sporadic, interrupted, complex, and intermittent for each of us, depending on our unique conditioning and psychological dynamics. From day to day, and depending on circumstances, the clarity, depth, and stability of the awakened perspective will inevitably ebb and flow. Some commentators have also suggested the useful distinction between waking up and growing up and stressed the importance of doing the psychological work of resolving the negative and dysfunctional conditioning and traumas of the past (growing up) that continue to limit our ability to embody our awakening in the here and now.

Pointer: Spiritual Bypassing

The concept of spiritual bypassing, formulated by the Buddhist psychologist John Welwood and now quite popular in spiritual circles, suggests that people who avoid confronting their unresolved psychological issues and emotional wounding and hide out exclusively in the awakened perspective can cause suffering for themselves and others.[5] Ignoring or downplaying their human limitations and shortcomings, they may use the language of the absolute–for example, awakened awareness is my natural state, and no effort, investigation, or practice is required to embody it–to excuse harmful behavior in everyday life. In particular, parts of the psyche that lurk in the shadows unacknowledged may rear their head and get acted out without conscious awareness.

Teachers who claim to be enlightened and have no needs may act out unconscious tendencies and habitual patterns by preying on their students to get those unacknowledged needs—for sex, power, or self-aggrandizement—met. Then, rather than taking responsibility and apologizing, they excuse their behavior by claiming that they have no self and therefore couldn't possibly have caused harm.

In this view, the way to avoid bypassing is by engaging in the two tracks of waking up and growing up—that is, discovering and embodying the truth of your nondual spiritual nature while becoming aware of your shadow and healing the wounds of childhood. The two can go hand in hand, but doing one without the other may lead to a kind of self-deception and gaslighting that causes suffering for all concerned.

On the other hand, it may be helpful at times to bypass the extensive psychological work of acknowledging and redeeming your shadow, at least temporarily, as you make waking up your primary focus. After all, this is the direct approach. Once you've awakened to some degree, you can turn the clarity of awakened awareness back upon the dream character you take yourself to be and focus on identifying and releasing the conditioning of a lifetime. (For more on deconstructing the dream, see chapter 6.)

The Three Stages of Dzogchen

One final framework I often teach for understanding the awakening process is known as "hitting the essence in three phrases," formulated by Garab Dorje, a legendary figure in Tibetan Buddhism considered to be the first person to receive the full Dzogchen teachings. I studied and practiced this framework with a well-known Tibetan teacher in the 1980s. In the first step, the teacher points you to the nature of mind (your natural state of awakened awareness), and you have a clear and definitive glimpse under their guidance. In the second, you clarify and deepen your realization, make it your own, and allow it to ripen into a genuine and irrefutable awakening. Finally, you "gain confidence through liberation" by discovering how living from this awakened perspective frees you from the conflictive emotions and reactivity that cause suffering.[6]

Once you have a clear and definitive glimpse, the next step is to allow and encourage it to clarify, ripen, and deepen, as Garab Dorje recommends. As doubts and misunderstandings that obscure the truth drop away, you're able to appreciate the nature of reality with greater and greater depth and subtlety, and you can abide in the recognition for extended periods of time without falling back into dualistic thinking or habitual reactive patterns. In the Tibetan tradition, only a person whose depth, clarity, and stability are perfect and unsurpassed can be considered a Buddha, a fully enlightened one. The rest of us are on the time-honored journey of a bodhisattva, an "awakening being."

What About Enlightenment?

Though Buddhism is the tradition that most clearly articulates the awakening process—in fact, Buddha means "awakened one"—there is no word in traditional Buddhism that distinguishes enlightenment from awakening. Generally, the Sanskrit term *bodhi*, which literally means "awakening," is used to refer to both (if in fact there is a distinction between them), except in the case of the Buddha, the fully enlightened one himself, for whom the term *samyaksambodhi*, "complete and perfect bodhi," is reserved.

The word "enlightenment" seems to have entered common parlance in the West in the late nineteenth century through the work of Buddhist scholars like Max Müller and was popularized by Beat writers in the fifties and sixties as a translation of the Zen terms *satori* and *kensho*. Most Zen texts and teachings in English use the word in this way. Tibetan Buddhists rarely use the English word "enlightenment" except to refer to the historical Buddha and the great masters like Padmasambhava or Milarepa.

The contemporary Tibetan teacher Dzigar Kongtrul defines enlightenment as "the state of mind of a buddha, one who has awakened to their ultimate potential. It is the most positive state of mind possible—a state of perfect, irreversible happiness and perfect, irreversible freedom from suffering."[7] In this state, all defilements of the mind have been abandoned and all excellent qualities and realizations have been completed.

In my experience, most people who have a powerful and irreversible shift in the locus of their identity (as described in chapter 1) don't end up in some permanently clear or abiding state of perfect freedom from confusion, anger, fear, attachment, or reactivity. Rather, as I explained in the previous section, awakening seems more often to be followed by a lifelong journey of deepening, clarifying, and embodying the truth to which we have awakened, accompanied by a compassionate welcoming of our experience, positive or negative, just as it is. (For more on welcoming, see chapter 7, page 149). There is no static end state, as the term "enlightenment" seems to imply, but an "endless awakening" to the depths and subtleties of Being. For this reason, I prefer the more neutral and descriptive term "awakening."

Reflect and Inquire

If you've experienced some awakening, where do you imagine you are on the trajectory described in this chapter? Have you had the intuitive recognition that you're not your thoughts and feelings but the one who is aware of them? If not, what are the stories, beliefs, and identities that you take to be who you are and that get in the way of recognizing your true nature as awareness itself?

If you've had glimpses of the awake awareness that's prior to all content, what, if anything, keeps you from recognizing that this awareness is who you really are, free of the dream person you take yourself to be? Spend ten minutes or more inquiring by asking yourself two questions and then taking several minutes to respond. If you find it helpful, you can speak your answers into a cell phone recorder or write them down: Who do I take myself to be? Then: Who am I really? Notice all the many identities and roles you're attached to that keep you from releasing into your natural state of inherent wakefulness. Would you be willing to let them go and rest in the openness prior to any identification?

Q&A

Q: You mention that some people may receive a download of wisdom that may take months or years to unpack. How does this unpacking occur?

A: In my own case, the awakening happened so suddenly and beyond the grasp of the conceptual mind that I was thrust into a deep and groundless silence that had no words. Only later did I realize that I had seen through all division and sense of separation in an instant, as when lightning illuminates the darkness in a flash, only to have everything return to darkness. Once I got caught in identification and separation again, as almost inevitably happens, I found myself going back over the dream and deconstructing it more gradually, in essence delving in a more granular way into the realization I'd already had. This is a common occurrence: The initial realization may include all the stages at once but can't be fully digested in the moment and must be reconsidered and gradually assimilated.

Q: As a starting point, you say most of us identify with our thoughts and feelings and take ourselves to be the story of our lives. On awakening, we realize that knower and known, awareness and its objects, are not separate. If our thoughts and feelings are the known, inseparable from the knower, are we not in a sense still identifying with the contents? How is it different?

A: First of all, you've left out the most important step, the recognition that you're the context free of the contents, the knower free of the known. This is the initial kensho that frees you from identification with the story of your life. The intimacy or inseparability that dawns when you finally see that awareness and its objects are not two doesn't involve psychological identification. It's the much more direct and existential recognition that you're inseparable not only from your thoughts and feelings but from everything you encounter. There's no space or distance between, there's just this one reality manifesting in a multiplicity of forms. Just This!

Meditation: Waking into the Nondual

The first stage of spiritual awakening is to recognize that you are not any of the content that arises in your awareness, not your thoughts or feelings or the stories you tell yourself about who you are. This insight is often the result of practicing some form of awareness meditation.

The next stage is to awaken to what you actually *are*: pure awareness, pure subjectivity, the context in which all the contents of awareness arise. This often sudden and surprising recognition is the initial kensho mentioned in the Zen koans.

But as amazing and transformative as this realization may be, it's still inherently dualistic–pure awareness here and all those objects over there.

The final stage of awakening, and the fruition of the spiritual journey, is the recognition that awareness and the objects of awareness, self and other, context and content, that which is looking and that which is looked at, are nondual, not separate, not two.

In this meditation I'll lead you on a journey through the stages of awakening, beginning with the foundational meditation of resting as awareness and allowing everything to be as it is, followed by awareness awakening to itself as the boundaryless openness in which all experience arises, and culminating in the recognition of the nondual nature of reality.

Begin by sitting quietly and allowing your body to settle. Rest your awareness on the coming and going of your breath for a few minutes.

Now let go of the focus on the breath and allow your awareness to naturally expand to include the full range of experience both inside and outside your body. Allow thoughts and feelings, tension and relaxation, pleasure and pain, to naturally arise and pass away as you allow your experience to be just as it is.

No need to intervene or change things in any way. Just resting in awareness and allowing experience to be as it is.

Notice that you're aware of these experiences but not caught up in them. You are not your thoughts or feelings or sensations, you are the one who is aware, though you may not yet know who this one is. Just rest and allow.

Now reflect on awareness itself. Notice the awake, aware space, the boundaryless, nonlocatable openness, that's prior to experience and allows experience to be. It can never be an object of experience itself, because it is the ultimate subject of all objects, the ultimate experiencer prior to all experience. It is what is always already looking through your eyes and experiencing through your senses.

Just rest as this boundaryless openness without center or periphery. You are this pure and limitless openness, the ground in which all experience arises. You can't experience it, but you can be it knowingly.

Now open your eyes and gaze at the objects around you from this newfound perspective of being the awareness, rather than being the separate self. What do you see? Are the objects around you solid and separate, or are they made of the same awareness, the same consciousness, that's gazing out through these eyes? Do they have any separate substantiality apart from the awareness with which they're perceived? What do you discover?

Gaze with sheer awareness into sheer awareness, and allow the usual constructs and concepts that organize your experience to dissolve in pure perception. No one perceiving, nothing perceived, only perceiving. Inside and outside, subject and object, not two.

Rest here for as long as you like, and when you feel complete, get up and go about your day.

3

Preparing the Path

Not long after I began practicing Zen single-mindedly, in a little zendo in a converted garage not far from Stanford University, the teacher, a young Japanese priest fresh from the monastery, gathered together a few of his closest students to study the sixteen precepts of Zen. I knew that Buddhism recommended ethical conduct but was surprised that we were taking the precepts so seriously so early in our Zen training. The orientation surprised me even more—instead of teaching them as prescriptions for conduct imposed from some authoritative source, the teacher emphasized that, at the deepest level, they were in fact just descriptions of how a truly awakened person would act. As the result of the nondual realization that inside and outside, self and other, are not two but an inseparable one, he implied, an awakened person would naturally not kill, steal, lie, or take advantage of others. At a more practical level, he added, when you act in unkind and self-serving ways, it agitates the mind and stirs up negative emotions, making meditation and awakening more difficult.

In the West these days we tend to stumble upon the pathless path and the nondual wisdom teachings without the ethical foundation that students would ordinarily have received in their traditional culture of origin. If you grew up in traditional Thailand, Tibet, or Japan, for example, you imbibed these ethical dos and don'ts from an early age and were expected to act in accord with them. In addition, as a spiritual acolyte, you would be taught rules of conduct appropriate to the monastic setting or the life of a devoted layperson. In contemporary societies both East and West, by contrast, ethics and the religions that teach them are in steady decline, as the corruption now so rife in the corporate and political spheres reveals, and we don't have the same ethical groundwork when we come to the spiritual search.

Because we're accustomed in our digital culture to instant gratification, we expect to have immediate access to these profound pointers and practices without any preparation whatsoever, merely because we're interested and can connect to the internet. There we can find videos and books by teachers of Zen, Dozgchen, or Advaita Vedanta offering wisdom that seekers would have had to wait and prepare for years to receive. But just because you can receive them doesn't mean you're ready to digest and assimilate them and make them your own. First you need to prepare the ground by clarifying your commitment and aspiration and learning to live in alignment with some deeper sense of purpose and integrity.

As a teacher of awakening for many years, I've found that certain preliminary practices and attitudes of mind and heart foster genuine awakening and make it more available to us. In the absence of these preliminaries, the powerful pointers I discuss in chapter 4 may fall like precious seeds on rocky soil and never take root. Or to use another metaphor, I find that people often arrive at the teachings half baked and unready and could use a little cooking or at least preheating first. In the nondual traditions such preparation was considered an essential part of the path and could take a number of forms. Of course, these preliminaries may appear to turn the direct approach into a more progressive endeavor, but in fact they're not necessary, only helpful, and they don't take you on a journey to somewhere other than where you are right now. (For more on the difference between direct and progressive approaches, see chapter 4.) In this chapter, we will look at the traditional preliminaries and their contemporary alternatives.

Traditional Preliminaries on the Pathless Path

In Asia, where these nondual wisdom traditions originated, the path of awakening and the teachings that led to it were (and often still are) largely reserved for monastics and, with rare exceptions, for highly motivated laypeople. If you wanted to wake up, you left your work and family, shaved your head (or grew your hair long and matted), went off to sit at the feet of a teacher, and spent long hours in contemplation and self-inquiry. If you were a wandering sadhu or monk, laypeople would offer you food and other forms of sustenance, or you would enter a community that worked together to support itself. The path of awakening was considered a noble endeavor that benefited the wider community with its insight and compassion and its emphasis on the sacred dimension of life, and that benefited from the community in turn through the respect and support it received.

In this more traditional framework, whether lay or renunciate, you would be encouraged or even required to engage in a series of preliminary practices and rituals that prepared you for the concerted meditation and self-inquiry you might expect to practice for years before your awakening blossomed. These preliminaries were intended to test and clarify your resolve and motivation, invite you to reflect on your aspirations for awakening, turn your heart toward the greater good, and clear away some of the negative habits that might hinder you on the path. Admittedly, these preliminaries were generally part of a progressive path of gradual realization rather than a direct path culminating in sudden awakening. As I explain later, however, the direct approach is often offered as the rarefied higher teachings of a progressive path within an established tradition.

As an example of what these preliminaries might look and feel like from the inside, I offer this brief tour of my years of Zen practice in the United States, leading up to my ordination as a monk and beyond. Other traditions differ, of course, but many of the basics are similar.

Though I was quite young when I began, I was already motivated by the suffering I had experienced in childhood to leave behind my other commitments and focus my attention on spiritual awakening. Like the revered Zen master Dogen, founder of the tradition in which I practiced, I had been introduced to impermanence by the loss of my mother at an early age. After beginning Zen practice on the East Coast, I moved to California with the express purpose of positioning myself to enter a monastery in the mountains not far away.

After a year of regular meditation practice every morning and evening, plus several long retreats, I set off for an extended period of intensive monastic practice and was met with the first demanding preliminary. To receive permission to enter the monastery, I had to sit in silence for seven days on a meditation cushion (no chairs allowed) in an anteroom outside the gates. No teachings, no walking, no group support, just nonstop sitting, with bathroom breaks, three light meals, and a brief night's sleep each day. This was a modern version of the time-honored practice of requiring an aspirant to wait outside the monastery gate whatever the weather and beg to be admitted. During this time you were expected to endure the heat and cold and reflect deeply on your motivation and your commitment to the path of awakening. After seven days of being refused, you would reluctantly be accepted as an acolyte—and immediately put to work.

Once I entered, even though I wasn't ordained yet, I was required to shave my head, which in those days of long hair was a symbolic act of renunciation declaring that I was giving up my preoccupation with worldly concerns. After each period of meditation in the zendo we chanted bodhisattva vows in which we dedicated our lives to discovering our true nature and benefiting all beings, reinforcing and deepening our motivation. Between periods of sitting we bowed repeatedly—toward the cushion that supported us, toward one another, toward the Buddha on the altar—strengthening our dedication and devotion. Indeed, my first Zen teacher used to say that Buddhism is a religion not of meditation, but of bowing—and by implication of surrender.

In addition, the rigors of monastery life were themselves preparation for awakening. The hard manual labor, the freezing winter nights in the meditation hall without heat, the sweltering summer days—these all pointed to the recognition that, as one teacher put it, there are no easy chairs anywhere, no comfort in the material world. Sitting long hours in meditation was a preliminary as well, pruning off the tangled branches of distorted, self-centered thinking in preparation for seeing the morning star of awakened awareness with utmost clarity.

Several years later, after I'd left the monastery, my teacher and I agreed that it was time for me to ordain as a monk while continuing to live and work in the world. Once again I shaved my head, and during the ceremony—known as *shukke tokudo* (literally, "leaving home and entering the Way")—I received the sixteen bodhisattva precepts and took refuge in the Three Jewels of Buddhism: Buddha (teacher), Dharma (teachings or truth), and Sangha (community of fellow seekers and, more broadly, all beings). The intention of the ceremony was to renounce my attachments—to home, family, external gratification—and devote my life to the journey. With a cleanly shaved head and new robes, I felt like a newborn baby starting out fresh, without the baggage of the life I had led to that point. Like similar ceremonies throughout the world's spiritual traditions, it was meant to initiate me into a new way of being and a whole new world of meaning.

After all the rituals and practices, I had become a completely different person from the hesitant and conflicted one who had begun the journey years before. The long hours and days of meditation—the most powerful preparation of all—accompanied by all the chanting, vowing, and bowing had honed my resolve and turned my life single-mindedly toward discovering the truth of my essential nature.

In the Tibetan Buddhist tradition, after taking refuge in the Three Jewels and receiving bodhisattva vows, the sincere student will generally engage in an extended series of preliminary practices known as *ngondro*—one hundred thousand whole-body prostrations and an equal number of guru-yoga visualizations, mandala offerings, and Vajrasattva mantra recitations and visualizations—that may take as long as ten years or more to complete. Only then can you receive the highest nondual teachings of Dzogchen and Mahamudra. In the Vedanta tradition you might be required to chant a special mantra and serve your guru for years before you could receive the direct pointers of Advaita.

Today, in both East and West, of course, very few of us have the time, resources, and community support to devote our lives to self-realization in this way. Most of us are busy making a living and supporting ourselves and our families and so must do our seeking on the side—or integrate it into our everyday lives. If you're lucky, you might be able to find the time to sit quietly or listen to a guided meditation for ten to twenty minutes in the morning and read a little or watch a video teaching after a long day of work. For those few who do have the time and a sincere wish to practice and engage in the extensive preliminaries, there are very few residential options available in the West to allow it, and most seekers need to carve out their own practice opportunities right where they live.

My intention in describing these preparatory practices and rituals in some detail is not to suggest that most of us should be engaging in them in the traditional way, even if we could, but to give a sense of the rich cultural and religious context out of which these precious nondual teachings have emerged and encourage us to consider finding alternative ways of preparing the ground. In my experience as a teacher, I find that many people stumble upon the pathless path with conflicting motivations, attitudes, and interests that work at cross-purposes and make the journey so much more difficult. In the next section I offer a series of pointers and questions to help you reflect on what you're up to and on how best to approach the journey in a more cohesive and wholehearted way.

Pointer: Practice What, and by Whom?

If pure wakefulness is your natural state, as close to you as breath itself and never apart from you even for a heartbeat, why should you need to practice it? But if you don't practice it, how can you recognize it, activate it, clarify it, and make it your own? Rinpoches, roshis, and sages have been debating this point for many hundreds of years.

The direct approach emphasizes that you're already awake and need merely join the inherent wakefulness that's always already taking place. In the words of Ramana Maharshi, "Practice what, and by whom? You alone exist." The progressive approach insists that wakefulness isn't innate but must be cultivated and practiced diligently lest it elude your grasp. Many Buddhist traditions combine both perspectives, practice and no practice, depending on where you are on the trajectory of awakening.

In the Tibetan tradition, years of practice are traditionally required to receive the direct pointing that reveals the truth to you. But are those years of diligent practice necessary after all, now that Dzogchen teachers have begun revealing the deepest truths successfully to those who haven't done the practices? No one knows for sure, though some teachers certainly have their opinions. You can only pursue the teachings and practices that appeal to you and find out for yourself.

Attitudes of Mind and Heart That Lay the Groundwork for Awakening

The nondual wisdom tradition teaches that awakened awareness is your natural state, the nondual presence that's always already experiencing life through this body and mind. Awakening is simply a matter of turning awareness back upon itself and recognizing and living as this awareness. Awakening can happen in a heartbeat, in any moment out of time—and at the same time, paradoxically, it's a journey that can take a lifetime to fully realize and embody, fraught with inner obstacles, habitual patterns, conflicting emotions, and deep-seated confusion.

Likewise, nothing is required to wake up, it's always available to you—and at the same time certain attitudes of mind and heart have been recommended throughout time by the great masters and sages to help catalyze this awakening. As a teacher, I'm fully aligned with those who say there's nowhere to go, nothing to do, and nothing to achieve, and at the same time I appreciate, from my own experience and my work with students, the years of dedication, energy, and commitment that are often required. As a result, I recommend some or all of the following attitudes.

Trust in the Teacher, Teachings, and Practices

Most often we're drawn to teachings about the nature of reality that we resonate with and intuitively know to be true. What we're looking for is a way to fully realize and embody these teachings and an awakened teacher to guide us in the process. After checking out and choosing to work with a particular teacher, the next step is to trust in their wisdom, set aside our doubts, and open our hearts and mind to receive what they offer. (For more on guidelines to follow in choosing and working with a teacher, see chapter 5.)

The same applies to the meditation and self-inquiry practices—they're time-honored methods for cracking us open and revealing the deeper truth beyond the mind, and we need to trust that they will work as prescribed, as they have in the past for those who came before us. I once had a student who claimed he trusted only scientific evidence, and when I asked whether he would trust his own direct experience unmediated by the mind, he said no. We ended up agreeing that he was probably on the wrong path, since the only reliable guidance on the pathless path comes from the still small voice within, not the mind.

Self-Compassion

Extending loving-kindness and compassion, especially to ourselves, is a fundamental practice in the Buddhist tradition, and much has been written in recent years on its many psychological benefits. I find self-compassion to be especially relevant on the path of awakening because the drive to relieve our suffering can be so intense that we may push ourselves too hard to be perfect and end up causing ourselves even more suffering. Particularly problematic is the common tendency to judge our progress and compare ourselves unfavorably to some spiritual ideal. "Why don't I have the realization of Ramana Maharshi, Longchenpa, Dogen Zenji, or more contemporary teachers like Mooji or Adyashanti?" we may complain. Or "Why haven't I solved as many koans as the monk sitting next to me in the zendo?" Just as awakening leads to greater self-acceptance and compassion, self-compassion supports us on our journey and protects us from inflicting more suffering on ourselves.

Meditation: Self-Compassion

In the traditional Buddhist practice known as *metta*, or loving-kindness, you begin by focusing your attention on your heart and imagining someone who loved or loves you unconditionally, perhaps a grandparent or close family friend. Notice the feelings of love this image evokes, and rest there for a few moments.

Now imagine someone *you* love and extend this same love to them from your heart, accompanied by phrases like "May you be happy. May you be healthy. May you be peaceful. May you have ease and well-being. May you be filled with loving-kindness."

Continue to extend this loving-kindness to others in your life, and conclude with extending it to yourself, which many people find the most difficult part of the practice. Imagine yourself filled and surrounded by love.

Once you learn how to do metta, you can apply it to yourself as needed when you feel ill, agitated, alone, or unloved. Love is what you are in essence—you just need to activate and share it.

Humility and Surrender

Once you realize that you're not in control of your life, and in fact the separate self you thought controlled your life doesn't really exist, true surrender and humility naturally arise in the face of the mystery that does in fact orchestrate the unfolding. Some helpful mantras here might be "let go and let it unfold" or "not my will but thy will be done." Until you have this realization, you can practice letting go of the illusion of control by noticing and relaxing any clenching in the body when you try to hold on, and by seeing and dropping the stories of struggle and conflict that the mind keeps generating. In the absence of thoughts to the contrary, is there a problem right now that you need to solve?

Dedication, Devotion, and an Awakened Heart

Devotion to a particular teacher and teachings, as well as dedication to the path itself, are fundamental heart qualities that fuel the journey. At their core is the principle known in Buddhism as *bodhichitta* (literally, "awakened heart-mind")—the deep wish for the benefit and well-being of others. As we become intimately attuned through our own experience to the suffering of the human condition, we may feel naturally moved to dedicate our lives to freeing all beings from it. Considered an innate human quality that can be revealed and cultivated, bodhichitta fuels the awakening process by connecting us to our deepest motivation as awakening beings (bodhisattvas) on the pathless path.

In my experience, bodhichitta is the warm, moist, and fertile soil in which the precious seeds received from the teacher and teachings sprout and bear fruit. It's innate to our heart but may need to be recognized and encouraged. Without this love and dedication as the ground, the seeds may fail to grow, and the awakening journey may sputter to a halt. The infinite, endlessly unfolding awakening I mention in the final chapter refers in part to this continued dedication to going deeper and deeper for the benefit of all beings.

Wholehearted Engagement

Out of bodhichitta naturally arises the energy, passion, and wholeheartedness that motivate us to keep going when we feel frustrated, disappointed, distracted, or drawn off course. Desire sometimes gets a bad rap in the spiritual traditions, but the desire for awakening transcends personal attachment and expresses the deep wish of our true nature to awaken to itself through us for the benefit of all. As one anonymous sage put it, that which you are seeking is always seeking you. Our personal aspirations are just an expression of an impersonal movement toward an ever greater revelation of the love and light at the heart of existence, which may be experienced as a deep and insistent calling from within.

Though we may recommend ease and effortlessness, the truth is that most masters and sages who have awakened to their true nature have done so after concerted and dedicated investigation and inquiry, whether it was the Buddha, who engaged in extreme austerities for many years before vowing to sit as long as necessary to realize his true nature; Ramana Maharshi, who gave himself over completely to death when it beckoned, then spent several years without moving while he integrated his realization; or Nisargadatta Maharaj, who says he believed what his teacher told him and practiced it unceasingly for three years until he woke up himself. Rare and blessed are those who wake up suddenly and spontaneously without any seeking, though most end up spending years devoted to integrating what they've discovered.

In the monastery we chanted this reminder from Eihei Dogen: "Life and death are of supreme importance. Time swiftly passes by and opportunity is lost. Each of us should strive to awaken. Awaken! Take heed, do not squander your life." In Theravada Buddhist monasteries monks and nuns meditate in cemeteries and outdoor areas where corpses are left to decompose as a reminder of death and impermanence and as a spur to wholehearted motivation. But you don't need to go to a cemetery to remember the loved ones you've lost and your own vulnerability and mortality during times of serious illness or other life-threatening events. These reminders are all around us.

My teacher Jean Klein used to call this wholehearted attitude "earnestness," and the Buddha likened it to tuning a stringed instrument: If you don't make the strings tight enough, you don't get any sound, but if you tighten them too much, they break and the instrument becomes useless. Using surfing as a metaphor, my first Zen teacher, Suzuki Roshi, counseled us to "follow the wave, drive the wave." That is, the wave will carry you most of the time if you let it, but sometimes you may need to exert effort to catch it. As the word "heart" suggests, this approach to the path wells up naturally from within, as an expression of what Suzuki Roshi called "our innermost request."

True Renunciation

As I described earlier, renunciation may traditionally take the form of relinquishing your worldly involvements and devoting yourself single-mindedly to a particular path. In the yoga tradition, you might practice *pratyahara*, withdrawal of the senses from external objects to focus awareness exclusively within. In the Buddhist tradition, you might shave your head, don the robes (which were originally rags), and face a wall for hours on end.

But the deeper sense of authentic renunciation is to give up expecting that anything outside yourself—any person, thing, relationship, career, status, or accomplishment—will bring you the lasting peace and happiness you seek. You acknowledge and vow that genuine fulfillment can only come from the realization of your nondual spiritual nature and the love, happiness, and peace of mind it evokes. You don't need a special ceremony to take this vow, you can make it to yourself and keep returning when you get lost in attachment and longing.

Beginner's Mind

When I teach, I inevitably say that I hope you'll leave knowing less than when you came. The point of all these teachings and practices is not to add to your store of conceptual knowledge but to strip you of what you think you already know and open you to the mystery of what is. As a preliminary attitude, you can keep this pointer in mind and read and listen to teachings not to figure things out or even become wiser and more knowledgeable, but to return you to your primordial awareness prior to knowing, your natural state of inherent wakefulness, which is identical to not knowing or beginner's mind.

Living in Alignment with Truth

The path of awakening requires a commitment to truth at every level, not just the absolute truth of the nondual nature of reality, but the relative truth in all its minute particulars. If you're dedicated to self-realization but continue to bullshit or deceive yourself and others, the light of awakening won't penetrate to the darkest recesses of your life and transform it from the inside. Keep this in mind as you start out on the pathless path: In the end it will require of you the utmost integrity, and you will need to die to all your illusions and be reborn to clarity of mind and heart. The commitment to truth is a purifying fire that ultimately consumes all the illusion and falsehood in its path.

The more deeply you see into the nature of reality, the deeper will be your commitment to aligning with the truth at every level, because you realize its power to free you and others from suffering. But even before awakening, you can make this commitment as an attitude you hold precious on the path and stay true to it with as much clarity as you can muster.

The English word "integrity" derives from the Latin for wholeness and implies this alignment with the truth of your being and the wholeheartedness and earnestness described in the previous section. This commitment to integrity is the pathless-path equivalent of the precepts of Zen or other traditions. If you continue to pursue truth but act without integrity in your everyday life, the inner conflict and division and the agitation of mind and heart it causes will come back to haunt you and ultimately sabotage the whole awakening enterprise. As one Western Buddhist teacher likes to joke, you can't meditate well after a day of lying and stealing, though I've certainly met people who try.

Be unflinching and uncompromising, but at the same time compassionate with yourself, recognizing your limitations with love and bearing witness to your experience at every level. Inner division and conflict are inevitable characteristics of the human condition, and it takes great courage to acknowledge and confront them. (For more on the multiplicity of selves, see chapter 7.) Don't try to impose some outside agenda or force yourself to live up to some spiritual standard foisted on you by others, but at the same time don't ignore the promptings of your own heart.

The truth you align yourself with may derive from some deep and intuitive inner knowing or from awakened awareness itself. Whatever your level of understanding, the journey of awakening requires complete transparency and a willingness to face the facts without defensiveness or obfuscation and take responsibility for your actions. Often we tell lies or stretch the truth because we feel we need to control the outcome of situations and the other people involved. Hence telling the truth means having the courage to give up (the illusion of) control. Living with integrity supports your awakening process, and awakening inevitably deepens your integrity in turn.

Commitment to Clarity of Mind and Heart

Without being puritanical or obsessively attached to some spiritual ideal, I recommend committing yourself to noticing how certain habitual actions and involvements affect the clarity of mind and devotion of heart that expedite your journey on the path of awakening. You can't live in alignment with the truth at every level if your mind isn't clear enough to discern what's true.

In particular, many of us these days are addicted to substances like alcohol, tobacco, pharmaceuticals, cannabis, or sugar that cloud the mind and dull or alter the senses and then wonder why awakening hasn't happened to us. This isn't a matter of right or wrong, it's a question of fearlessly observing and confronting the ways we're conflicted and work at cross-purposes with ourselves.

For example, I had a client who professed to be deeply committed to the awakening process, only to reveal that he smoked a joint or two throughout each day to stay continuously high. When I pointed out this apparent contradiction, he seemed ashamed and apologetic and vowed to give it up going forward. I told him to contact me when he'd stopped using, but I never heard from him again. Is it possible to wake up while actively using cannabis? Perhaps. But does it help you on your way? Almost certainly not, and those who think it does are, in my experience, generally deluding themselves, no doubt helped by the fog of THC. Likewise with the other substances. Honestly check out how they affect you day to day and ask, are they hindering or expediting my awakening? And if they are a hindrance, what can I do about it?

At an even more granular level, you may want to inquire into the ways you're using your attention from moment to moment and notice your addiction to certain mind-states or experiences. For example, do you profess to be committed to peace of mind and heart but keep watching pornography or violent TV or movies, or reading about politics or world affairs obsessively in ways that increase your agitation or fear? Addiction to the contents of the mind—and particularly to certain beliefs and points of view—may be the most pernicious addiction of all.

As for psychedelics like LSD, psilocybin, MDMA, and their cousins, I find that they may have the value of jolting us out of the bubble we've created for ourselves and opening us up to a deeper reality beneath the apparent world of manifestation. For people who seem stuck in repetitive thought patterns and constant self-judgment, I'll occasionally recommend a medicine journey. Ultimately, psychedelics are just pointers to a more integrated and abiding understanding. They're not meant to be a substitute for the ongoing work of recognizing, returning to, and resting in awareness from moment to moment.

Making Informed Lifestyle Choices

Though he rarely offered recommendations on how to live, my teacher Jean Klein would occasionally offer this advice to his students: If possible, work no more than three or four days a week, and the rest of the time "live in beauty," by which he meant enjoy the subtler pleasures of life—nature, the arts, good friends and family, and periods of silence and ease of being. The broader implication was that we would do well to harmonize our lives with our commitment to truth and not cause unnecessary stress and complication by focusing on achievement and material gain. Again, the primary point is to pay attention to how what we do with our time and what we consume at every level affects our state of mind and heart. No right or wrong here as well—and, as always, be kind to yourself. Jean thought of the process as a laboratory in which we could discover what worked best to support our realization. The rest was, and is, up to each of us.

Reflect and Inquire

Spend some time reflecting on your attitudes, motivations, and aspirations on the journey of awakening. Why would you possibly want to wake up when the process of awakening can be so unpredictable? What do you expect to realize or achieve? How long have you been engaged in the process? Are you motivated by a deep wish to relieve your suffering, satisfy your curiosity, accomplish some heroic quest, live up to some spiritual ideal? Or are you simply drawn by the inexpressible longing of the heart? Are you willing to go to the great lengths that Dogen and other masters and teachers describe?

It's often said that no effort is required to realize the awakened awareness that's always already present and available to us. Yet at the same time waking up may require a lifetime of dedication and devotion to the journey. Many of my students have spent decades pursuing full and genuine awakening. How long have you been engaged in the process? Are you ready and willing to give your life to it? Are you willing to renounce the expectation that the outside world will provide you the fulfillment you seek and take refuge in your own inner wisdom? As one of my teachers used to say, don't set out on the journey halfheartedly, because once you've begun, there's no turning back.

Q&A

Q: With so many different disciplines for spiritual growth, how do I know what practice and teacher to trust with such an important part of my life?

A: No one can tell you what's best for you, which is one of the reasons it's called the pathless path: There are no preestablished road markers and milestones to tell you whether you're on the right track. Only you can discern which direction to take based on your own inner knowing, and only you can hone your unique inner guidance system based on a lifetime of practice. In my experience, the best advice is to consult your heart rather than your mind and ask yourself the question, "How does love move me to act?"

Q: How, in practical terms, do I strike the right balance between effortlessness and concerted, dedicated investigation and inquiry? The two concepts seem contradictory. Is there a sweet spot between them that I should aim for? How do I know when I've landed in the best mindset for achieving awakening most efficiently?

A: First, there's nothing efficient about the process of waking up; you just fumble along, experimenting with different approaches and practices, following the guidance of a teacher (or not), until awakening finally dawns. You're not in control, and awakening is a kind of sacred accident. At the same time, as you suggest, you can give yourself to the process earnestly and wholeheartedly, not because you're stressing and straining, but because you make it your number one priority in this lifetime. Yes, there's a sweet spot. Remember this suggestion from the Buddha: If you tune the instrument too tight the strings snap, too loose and you get no sound.

Meditation: Global Awareness

Ordinarily we tend to focus or fixate our awareness on objects, including thoughts, emotions, other people, or things. But the essential nature of awareness isn't localized or fixed in any way. This meditation will introduce you to the natural state of awareness, which is open, boundaryless, and all inclusive.

Find a comfortable sitting position and allow your body to settle. Begin by noticing where your awareness is focused right now. For most people, awareness tends to be fixated in the forehead, in the thought factory in the neocortex.

Allow your awareness to gradually descend out of the head, through the neck and into the torso, and allow it to settle on the coming and going of your breath, the rising and falling of your chest and belly as you breathe.

Spend a few minutes being aware of your breath, not from above, but from inside the body, from inside the breath itself. Awareness rests intimately on the coming and going of your breath.

Now let go of the focus on the breath and allow awareness to naturally open, expand, and permeate the body. No focus, no fixation, no effort. Just be aware of the body as a field of sensation, not looking down from above, but being aware from inside the sensation itself.

Can you sense the edges of the body? Do they seem solid and fixed, or do they seem open and porous? Can you find a clear boundary between inside and outside? Can you really know where inside ends and outside begins?

Allow any remaining boundaries of your body to dissolve into the space around you. Inside and outside becoming one seamless, continuous field of sensation. Allow this space to continue opening and expanding far beyond the boundaries of the body to include sounds, smells, objects, other people. Everything is happening in this limitless space without edges or center. There's nothing you need to do. Just allow it to unfold.

Awareness is intrinsically boundless and boundaryless, open, all-inclusive, above, below, right and left, front and back, extending infinitely in every direction. It's like the sky. Everything is included in its boundaryless embrace, nothing is left out.

As the boundaries and the divisions dissolve, what happens to the localized sense of being a separate someone? Where are you located? Where do you leave off and the outside world begin? Just rest as this limitless space without edges or center and allow everything to unfold naturally without effort or interference. You are the awake, aware space in which everything arises and passes away. Nothing to attach to, nothing to reject.

Everything is arising and passing in you. Even the arbitrary separation between awareness and the objects arising in awareness falls away. There's only This, endlessly unfolding, endlessly revealing itself, vivid, aware, seamless, nondual.

Rest as this openness for as long as you like. When you feel complete, you can get up and go about your day.

4

The Direct Approach

After about ten years of facing a wall (both literally and figuratively) in intensive Zen meditation, with the goal of breaking through the gateless barrier described by the masters of old and realizing my true face before my parents were born, I stopped, put aside my monk's robes, left the monastery, got a job, and eventually went back to school to study Western psychology. I just couldn't continue on the path of relentless seeking to which I had dedicated myself because my efforts seemed increasingly futile and the goal of enlightenment (whatever that was) seemed further and further away. My meditation felt dry and lifeless, and I needed to step beyond the stuffy meditation cave I had carved out and rediscover the fresh air of ordinary life.

Half a dozen years later, after exploring Vipassana and Tibetan Buddhism and a variety of nonmeditative modalities and disciplines, I met a teacher of what he called the "direct approach" to spiritual awakening who taught that seeking for something we imagine we don't already have takes us further from what we already are. We merely need to take the backward step—so often talked about in Zen but not often clearly articulated—and recognize that consciousness, awake awareness, our natural state of nondual presence is already available to us.

During one of my first retreats with this teacher, Jean Klein, I found myself meditating as I always had, trying so hard to be aware, when it suddenly dawned on me that the bright light of consciousness was always shining, and struggling to be aware was like shining a flashlight at midday in the hope that it would make things brighter. I suddenly broke into uproarious laughter. This was my introduction to the direct approach.

Comparing the Direct and Progressive Approaches

Many spiritual traditions offer a progressive path, a set of clear-cut guidelines and techniques for developing specific qualities and abilities and achieving certain desirable states of mind or heart. In essence, these are self-improvement methodologies designed to enable us to progress slowly but steadily toward some spiritual ideal. If we practice mindfulness diligently, for example, we're told our mind will quiet down, we'll become more peaceful and less distracted, and we'll gradually develop insight into the nature of reality. If we cultivate loving-kindness, we'll develop heart qualities like equanimity, empathy, and compassion and become better human beings.

Progressive approaches like mindfulness can be exceptionally effective at delivering the self-improvement they promise. There's plenty of research over the past twenty years that demonstrates that the regular practice of mindfulness meditation reduces stress and anxiety, relieves depression, enhances the enjoyment of life, eases chronic pain, and increases emotional intelligence. It even reshapes the brain in significant beneficial ways. And it does this by encouraging an inner spaciousness that allows us to become aware of thoughts and feelings without immediately identifying with them or reacting to them.

But there are several problems or contradictions at the heart of progressive approaches that ultimately turn them from an asset into a hindrance on the path of awakening. At a certain point, the effort to maintain a certain state of mind (like being mindful) can begin to seem laborious and mechanical, and you may find yourself longing for a more spontaneous, less manipulative way of being present.

The emphasis on self-improvement may perpetuate the impression that you're flawed and inadequate as you are and need something from outside that you don't already have to complete yourself. This sets in motion an endless process of subtle striving and self-judgment and reinforces the very sense of inadequacy you may be working so hard to overcome. You keep asking yourself if you're becoming a better meditator or a more spiritual person, as you check your progress again and again. Instead of offering yourself the opportunity to shift from constant doing to the joy of just being, you allow your usual goal orientation to permeate your meditation—and, in turn, your life. This constant self-monitoring creates an inner split or duality between subject and object, watcher and watched, cat and mouse, that becomes deeply ingrained and very difficult to release.

In the same way, the deliberate practice of a technique like mindfulness may reify the apparent existence of a separate practitioner who needs to maintain awareness through constant effort. In fact, mindfulness practice requires a meditator at its core to keep it going, which in turn prevents you from relaxing into the realization that awareness requires no effort and is always taking place—or even more deeply that the separate self you take yourself to be is just an illusion and there is just this, nondual reality endlessly unfolding. (For a more thorough critique of mindfulness, see my book *Beyond Mindfulness*.)

In contrast to the progressive path, the direct approach teaches that there's nowhere else we need to go and no qualities we need to acquire. We already have the wisdom and compassion we seek, we just need to find a way to access them. Instead of cultivating some special faculty called awake awareness, we need merely turn our awareness back upon itself and recognize our natural state of inherent wakefulness, which is hidden behind layers of conditioning and belief just as the sun is hidden behind layers of clouds.

Rather than teaching us new spiritual beliefs to add to the ones we already have, as many progressive paths do, the direct approach challenges our most cherished assumptions and invites us to replace them with direct experience. Rather than using sustained effort to cultivate mind-states that contribute to happiness and peace of mind, it cuts to the heart of the matter and reveals the innate happiness and peace of mind we were born with but have lost touch with.

Instead of trying to build an edifice of cultivated qualities and states that are deemed more spiritual, the direct approach seeks to deconstruct the edifice of belief, interpretation, and emotion we've already constructed to reveal the innate perfection and completeness that lies at its core. In this way, it's truly radical because it cuts through the leaves and branches and takes us directly to the root, which is the illusion of duality and separation. Through guided meditations, dialogue, focused self-inquiry, and verbal pointers to the nature of reality, the direct approach seeks to elicit a direct realization of the nondual nature of reality, beyond the mind.

Practices like regular meditation have a place in the direct approach, but only as an invitation to recognize and rest in our inherent wakefulness, not as a means to achieve some different, supposedly more spiritual state of mind. There's no need to put another head on top of your own by cultivating mindfulness, as Zen warns. The boundaryless openness of nondual presence is always already available, you just need to turn your attention back upon itself and recognize it once and for all. The ongoing practice then becomes not creating a more mindful state, but recognizing, returning to, and resting in the effortless awareness that's always taking place.

Direct Pointing and Special Transmission in Zen

The term "direct approach," which I adopted from my teacher Jean Klein and now use to describe the teachings and practices I offer, dates back to the earliest years of the Zen tradition I practiced as a monk and can be applied to similar approaches in Dzogchen and Advaita Vedanta. The legendary master Bodhidharma, who purportedly brought Zen (along with tea plants) from India to China around 600 AD, sums up the direct approach in the famous aphorism traditionally attributed to him:

> A special transmission outside the scriptures,
> no dependence on words and letters.
> Pointing directly to the human heart/mind,
> see true nature (kensho), become Buddha.[1]

This description contains several of the essential elements of the approach—pointing, seeing, and transmission—and embodies its radical, revolutionary spirit, which rejects the words and letters that often obscure the truth and instead emphasizes direct experience.

The great masters of Tang dynasty China were notorious for using this direct pointing to elicit sudden awakenings, as a reading of the koan stories of Zen makes clear. Often the pointing occurred in unconventional and unexpected ways—the more unexpected the better so the student wouldn't see it coming and would be caught off guard and pushed beyond his or her comfort zone into a new way of experiencing. Here are a couple of well-known examples:

- A monk asked Ummon, "What is Buddha?" The master answered, "Dried shit."
- A monk asked Joshu why Bodhidharma came to China. Joshu said, "An oak tree in the garden."
- If you meet the Buddha on the road, kill him.
- Joshu asked his master Nansen, "What is the Way?" Nansen said, "Everyday mind is the Way." Joshu said, "Should we aim at this?" Nansen said, "The moment you aim at anything, you've already missed it."

- What is the sound of one hand?
- Does the dog have buddha nature? asked the monk. The master responded, NOT!

Some masters even resorted to violent, erratic behavior that we would not condone today but was considered more acceptable at the time, like killing a cat or cutting off a disciple's finger.

Of course, many of these masters also recommended the diligent practice of meditation, and the dialogue and rivalry between the sudden and gradual schools of Zen raged for centuries, until they eventually agreed that gradual cultivation through meditation and sudden awakening could coexist and intermingle. In other words, the rigorous practice of meditation might make you more awakening prone, but eventually you had to step off what one koan calls the "top of the 100-foot pole" of progress and fall into the complete openness and boundarilessness of true nature.

Perhaps the most famous exchange on the difference between direct and progressive paths and sudden and gradual awakenings occurs in the *Platform Sutra*, in which two monks vie to be the successor of the Fifth Zen Patriarch in China. The assembly of monks is invited to step forward one by one and express their understanding, but they defer to the head monk, Shen-hsiu, who writes this verse:

The body is the Bodhi tree,
The mind is like a clear mirror.
At all times we must strive to polish it,
And must not let the dust collect. [2]

In other words, we need to practice meditation diligently to maintain the awakened mind and heart we've revealed.

The Fifth Patriarch realizes this is not a fully awakened response but sits back and waits to see if someone emerges with a better understanding. In the dark of night, an illiterate young woodcutter who just arrived at the monastery galvanizes the community, and brings a smile to the patriarch's face, with his verse, posted on the wall with the assistance of one of the monks:

> Bodhi originally has no tree.
> The mirror has no stand.
> Buddha-nature is
> always clear and pure.
> Where is there room for dust?

Or, in another version:

> The mind is the Bodhi tree,
> The body is the mirror stand.
> The mirror is originally clean and pure;
> Where can it be stained by dust?[3]

In other words, the recognition that everything is innately perfect as it is—or, even more deeply, not only perfect but ungraspable and empty of substantiality—makes diligent, ongoing practice unnecessary. Nothing to change, nothing to achieve, everything is as it is! This response reverberated across the centuries and marked the difference between the direct and progressive approaches.

You Are the Path

At the heart of the direct approach is the understanding that no single methodology for realizing our essential spiritual nature is appropriate for everyone. In my own experience as a teacher, I've found that each person wanders along the pathless path in their own unique and inimitable way. Indeed, that's what makes it the pathless path—the seeker creates the path as they go, and they know before they begin that it's not taking them anywhere but right here and now. The teacher's job is to attune to where they are on their journey and help guide them back home, not impose some predetermined agenda for arriving somewhere else. In the words of the Thai Buddhist master Ajahn Chah, the guide's role is to notice how the student is moving along the path and say, maybe go a little left or go a little right. I've found that each journey has its own mysterious alchemy and serendipity, and all we can really do, as teacher and student, is align with it and help it on its way.

In this spirit, my friend and fellow Dharma teacher Stephen Levine used to call Advaita Vedanta the high path with no railing, because it lacks the structure and clear guidelines of the Vipassana tradition of which he was a part. He didn't mean this phrase as a criticism but as a caveat: Tread carefully, keep your balance, and be especially attentive, because you have a long way to fall.

If you choose to follow this high path, without the clear guardrails of the progressive approach, you'll be especially called upon to develop and fine-tune your discernment and inner guidance system for gravitating to the teachings and practices best suited for you. As I explain in the next section, the approach offers a number of skillful means for eliciting an awakening, and you're invited to experiment with the ones that resonate for you. Rather than becoming a dilettante, using your analytical mind to compare and contrast different teachers and teachings, sampling here and there but never going deep, I recommend listening for what you're authentically drawn to, contemplating it carefully and deeply, and letting it mature and ripen gradually in the crucible of your own heart. In the process of discernment, you may first have to set aside the alternative perspectives the mind keeps cranking out, which may all seem equally plausible but none convincing, and drop your attention out of the head and rest it in the heart with an attitude of openness and not knowing.

With so many nondual teachers and teachings vying for your attention these days, it's eminently possible to feel overwhelmed and confused, as do many of the people who end up coming to study with me. There are so many different and even contradictory ways of expressing the same basic, and ultimately very simple, truths, and it's easy for the mind to get lost in the concepts. I recommend keeping your intake of teachings simple, even austere, and leaving aside for now what doesn't resonate. As I often say when I teach, I hope you'll leave knowing less than when you came. In fact, simply reflecting upon and revealing the deeper meaning of a single teaching can cut through the mind's confusion and wake you up in a heartbeat.

Based on my own experience as both teacher and student, I would also extol the value of the teacher-student relationship and the consistent guidance that a single teacher can provide over many years of study and interaction. As they get to know you, and you familiarize yourself with their approach and learn to trust them, their words and presence can circumvent the mind's inherent resistance to recognizing your nondual spiritual nature. Hearing the same teachings and pointers again and again can have cumulative power, as the words gradually penetrate your habitual worldview and burst the bubble of your limited understanding. (For more on the value of a teacher and the teacher-student relationship, and some of the problems as well, see chapter 5.)

Pitfalls of the Direct Approach

The direct approach is not without its own pitfalls, of course. Perhaps the most glaring is the tendency among some adherents to cultivate a keen conceptual understanding of the basic tenets and use them as a substitute for genuine realization, a process I call Advaita-speak or Dharma logic. The direct approach teaches that there's no place else to go, nothing to attain but what we already have, nothing to cultivate because we already are what we're seeking—we merely need to discover it for ourselves. But this convenient formula can be easily reduced to the mistaken assumption, so often championed by a certain subset of teachers known as neo-Advaitins, that you're already awakened and no awakening experience or genuine shift in the locus of identity is required. This approach somehow bypasses the essential step of exploring, inquiring, and discovering these deeper truths directly for ourselves. Otherwise, the pathless path has disappeared, to be replaced by a kind of well-defended complacency.

Likewise, using the same easy formulas, the student may confuse the absolute and relative dimensions of being (see the pointer in this chapter) and excuse misguided or self-serving behavior by claiming there is no separate self to blame. This tendency is known as spiritual bypassing (see the pointer in chapter 2.) For example, one well-known teacher who espoused the view that doing just happens but there is no doer, when confronted by female students about his sexual advances, explained that he wasn't in charge of his actions and so couldn't be held accountable. In the same vein, some people claim that the anger, fear, or jealousy they're expressing is just illusory and couldn't possibly be a problem, even though it's clearly causing suffering for others. If everything is perfect as it is, they argue, then no behavior or emotion is unacceptable.

At the absolute or ultimate level, this may be true, but on the relative level of personal relationships and real-world functioning, there are clear-cut and widely held ethical norms and guidelines that we agree to adhere to in our interactions with others, in addition to the care we naturally apply based on our innate sensitivity and compassion.

In Zen, this mistaken claim that we're already enlightened and nothing need be done to recognize it is derided as "no matter Zen" and countered by the paradox of the gateless gate. Yes, the barrier separating us from the realization of our true nature may be an illusory one, and we already are intrinsically what we seek. But until we realize this truth directly for ourselves, we're caught outside the barrier and still need to pass through the gate to reap the transformative benefits of full realization. We may convince ourselves and others that our passivity is true surrender, when in fact it's merely resignation, confusion, and inertia.

If there's nothing to seek and we already are what we pretend to be seeking, then the search itself is paradoxical. Take the saying that the truth can't be found by seeking, but only seekers find it. It's not entirely true; of course, plenty of non-seekers stumble upon it, yet the earnest application and curiosity of the sincere seeker make awakening much more likely. If we push too hard, we may get caught in striving and perfectionism, but if we don't assert ourselves in any way, we may not make it out of the garage, as my teacher Jean Klein used to warn.

As a teacher of the direct approach, I also find that many people who are sincerely drawn to the nondual perspective are still so lost in their conceptual minds that they don't have room for the teachings. Like the professor in the famous Zen story whose cup of tea overflows,[4] their minds are brimming over with ideas and preconceptions and unable to receive fresh insight. Before I stumbled upon Jean Klein, who cautioned against using meditation as a means to an end outside ourselves, I spent more than ten years meditating intensively and becoming familiar with the agitation and repetitive patterns of my conceptual mind. Did those years of practice prepare me to hear and take to heart the nondual teachings? Without doubt they did, in particular by giving me some inner spaciousness and relief from the contents of my mind and by teaching me how to stay present for my experience for extended periods of time. For those who come to me with an overflowing cup, I will often recommend regular mindfulness meditation practice, with the caveat that they practice it not as a means to achieve some special state but as a way to familiarize themselves with their natural state of empty, open, awake awareness.

The Direct Approach and Its Cultural Context

Traditionally, of course, the direct approach came deeply embedded in a cultural context and symbol system that would take years of study and practice to become acquainted with and assimilate before you could get to the heart of the teachings. In the Tibetan Buddhist tradition, you would be expected (and still are with many teachers) to complete extensive preliminary practices involving one hundred thousand whole-body prostrations and an equal number of guru-yoga visualizations, mandala offerings, and Vajrasattva mantra recitations and visualizations before you received pointing-out instructions from a certified lama. In Zen you would generally spend years mastering the ritual, washing toilets or tending the garden, and counting or following your breaths before you advanced to koan study with the master.

At the same time, the teachings would be surrounded by esoteric symbols and references that acted as a kind of secret code or buffer that made them difficult to access or decipher. In the Tibetan tradition you would generally be expected to generate elaborate visualizations of certain deities and work with the mantras and energies associated with them along a gradual path leading to the so-called higher, or *maha ati*, teachings at the pinnacle of the path. In Zen, at least in its Japanese incarnation, you would need to practice and master complicated rituals and the formalities of monastery life and then crack the arcane code of the koan system, which is based on stories and references drawn largely from medieval China.

Of the three direct-approach traditions, Advaita has always been the most readily available to anyone who's drawn to study it. The core Advaita texts, the Upanishads, are perhaps the most succinct and accessible pointers to the essential unity at the heart of apparent duality, and the great Advaita teachers of the twentieth century—Ramana Maharshi, Nisargadatta Maharaj, Jean Klein, Atmananda Krishna Menon, and H. W. L. Poonja—opened their doors to whoever went in search of them. Perhaps because it's the most accessible and direct, many if not most of the contemporary nondual teachers in the West, whether they studied Advaita or woke up spontaneously on their own without a teacher or lineage, align themselves with it.

Over the centuries the barriers to the direct approach erected by Zen and Dzogchen have served their intended purpose of preparing neophytes to receive and comprehend the highest teachings while at the same time weeding out dilettantes and others with limited aspiration and dedication who might otherwise have exhausted the teacher without fully appreciating what they taught. (For the benefits of preparation, see chapter 3.) At the same time, though, these barriers have limited the number of people who could have benefited from the powerful truths they were intended to protect.

Now these once-secret and inaccessible teachings are widely available to anyone with a computer or smartphone who might be drawn to study them through retreats, webinars, videos, podcasts, and even apps. The potential benefits of this widespread access are obvious, but it does have risks and drawbacks. The first is that it reduces hard-won realizations to easy aphorisms and social-media caricatures that have no real transformative power and trivializes the deeper truths to which they refer. If not treated with the utmost reverence, these teachings can become just more consumable content in our voracious digital culture, to be swallowed whole and quickly spit out as we move on restlessly to something new. The second risk is that the genuine pathless path to ever-deeper realization may get replaced by the aimless meandering of the dilettante, who adds more and more teachers and teachings to their voluminous spiritual résumé but gets no closer to the transformative, and ultimately very simple and direct, spiritual awakening to which they originally aspired.

Pointer: The Mystery of Absolute and Relative

The major currents of the nondual wisdom tradition—Zen, Dzogchen, and Advaita Vedanta—share the view, known as the two truths, that this one indivisible reality has two dimensions or levels that are simultaneously and paradoxically true.

At the relative or individual level, we're separate people with unique characteristics, personalities, preferences, needs, desires, life stories, and points of view. Man or woman, liberal or conservative, rich or poor, old or young—these are the differences that distinguish us and set us apart in the everyday world of conventional discourse.

Simultaneously, at the absolute or universal level, we share the same essential nature, which is inherently awake, limitless, timeless, compassionate, and pure. When we're operating from this level, we know ourselves to be the vast ocean of being expressing itself through this particular form, and we recognize that the consciousness that gazes out through these eyes is the same as the one that gazes out through yours.

As we move through life, we may take things to be real in an ordinary, everyday way, while at the same time perceiving them to be nothing but spirit or consciousness, impermanent and empty of substantiality on the absolute level. The brown rice or burger I'm eating may be pure consciousness in manifestation, but it sure tastes good and satisfies my hunger. In fact, I couldn't make it through the day without it.

My teacher Jean Klein used to say that we exist at the juncture of the vertical and the horizontal—the absolute timeless Now and the relative movement of becoming through time and space. We're like Jesus, God incarnate, fixed to the center of the cross where divine and human meet.

Most people are unaware of the absolute level; it's what reveals itself to us when we awaken from the dream and realize our essential spiritual nature, beyond the mind. Even after it dawns, however, we may continue to feel like a confusing, and at times seemingly irreconcilable, blend of the two dimensions. We know who we are at a universal level, yet we still experience ourselves as a separate person, existing as a particular body-mind, drawn to particular people and situations and not others, having certain problems, plans, memories, emotions, values, and attachments unique to us.

The question is, which level do you identify with? If you identify with the relative alone, you suffer in the dream of separation. If you identify solely with the absolute, how do you function in the everyday world of intimate relationships and work without renouncing your humanness and indulging in spiritual bypassing? How does consciousness express itself through this form? The truth is, we're both levels simultaneously, an individual wave inseparable from the ocean of being. The ocean is our deepest ground, our essential nature, the ultimate source of all manifestation. Knowing ourselves to be the absolute is true freedom, the fruition of the spiritual search.

The dance of absolute and relative dimensions in each individual life unfolds in its own mysterious way. The challenge is to welcome them both and allow them to interact and interpenetrate naturally, to function as a separate human being while resting in the knowing that we are Being or consciousness itself. The two levels fit together like a box and its lid or two arrows meeting in midair, in the words of the famous Zen text "The Identity of Relative and Absolute."[5] But experientially it may often feel more like oil and water, never quite resolving into a smooth and integrated blend. Such is the vital and paradoxical mystery of the two truths.

Making Yourself Awakening Prone

Fortunately, the direct approach has its own collection of pointers and practices, some of them quite similar to those of the progressive approach, that can help facilitate genuine awakening. The difference lies not necessarily in the methods used, but in the view that underlies them and the way of applying them. Unlike the progressive way, the direct approach does not counsel that you can gradually make your awakening happen by following a set of prescribed practices. Rather, it views awakening as a kind of sacred accident that happens in its own unique and mysterious way, generally quite suddenly and without warning. But you can make yourself accident prone.

In chapter 3 I described the attitudes of mind and heart that can lay the groundwork for awakening. Here I offer some of the practices and other skillful means, drawn from my years of teaching and the classical sources that have informed and inspired me, that you can engage in to make it more likely to happen. Remember, traditional meditation techniques from the progressive approach may also be helpful (and even advisable) if practiced from a more direct-approach point of view, as long as you don't become attached to them and the outcomes they promise. Stay attuned to what teachings and practices appeal to you—and trust your intuition, heart wisdom, and inner knowing to guide you in the process, along with perhaps an experienced teacher to offer suggestions along the way.

The primary skillful means or methods of the direct approach include listening to, reflecting upon, and contemplating the pointers of awakened teachers and sages; practicing presence (essentially, resting in awareness and allowing experience to be as it is without judgment or intervention); self-inquiry and investigation of our essential spiritual nature; and spending time with a living teacher in the company of other like-minded spiritual seekers.

Pointing, Listening, Reflecting, Meditating

In the Vedanta tradition, of which Advaita is a part, students are instructed to listen carefully to the teachings and pointers of the guru, reflect upon and contemplate them deeply to resolve any doubts, and finally meditate upon the truths they've gleaned from these teachings until they realize them fully for themselves. My teacher Jean Klein used to say that the words of the teacher arise directly from truth and are imbued with the perfume of their source. Listening and contemplating transports you beyond the words and provides a direct portal back to your natural state of awakened awareness. This process requires patient and devoted application and takes place in silence without conceptualization, and this silence has its own intrinsic power that charges and infuses the words themselves.

In Zen these pointers are known as "turning words" that direct the mind toward the Dharma. In Dzogchen they're called "pointing-out instructions." Each tradition goes about this pointing in slightly different ways, as I describe in the remainder of this section. The key is that the pointers be accurate and facilitate a direct recognition of the truth to which they point. Once this recognition has occurred, the practice is to keep returning and resting there until it's fully realized and ultimately becomes your abiding perspective.

Zen Pointers

Koan collections are replete with teaching stories detailing the verbal pointers and instructive behaviors of the Zen masters of old. Some koans seem readily comprehensible even to the neophyte reader, whereas others require more extended reflection and contemplation to crack the code. The most challenging koans may take many years of intensive investigation in the meditation hall and under the guidance of an experienced teacher and still be slow to reveal their secrets. The truth is, many are written using a self-referential language and symbol system that has been passed down through the generations and that only seasoned Zen students steeped in this language can understand.

Zen makes an important distinction between live words and dead words. Live words are concise formulations rooted in the truth that have the power to turn our awareness back upon itself and wake us up to our true nature. Dead words are the ordinary expressions we use in everyday life to refer to the objective world that's apparently outside us. They are merely conceptual and lack awakening power but have a useful role to play in helping us understand the fundamental teachings and orienting us to where we are on the path. Live words generally constitute the "punch line" of a Zen koan, the expression that jolts the disciple out of their habitual way of perceiving reality into a new way of knowing. A teacher's job is to offer live words as much as possible, leaving the mind of the student no way to intervene.

Advaita Pointers

In the direct approach, pointing out is the teacher's most important function. Simply by perceiving, acting, and speaking from the awakened perspective, the teacher offers a radical critique of our conventional, dualistic worldview and keeps directing our attention again and again to nondual presence beyond the conceptual mind. The more time we spend in the presence of an awakened teacher, with or without words, and the more we're willing to engage them in dialogue, the more pointers we'll receive. Jean Klein called our group gatherings simply "dialogues," and the answers he offered to the questions I posed ultimately cut through the mind's defenses and woke me up.

The sacred texts of Advaita Vedanta are known as Upanishads, which literally means "sit down next to" in Sanskrit, referring to the importance of the teacher-disciple relationship and the traditional practice of imbibing pointers at the feet of the guru. Nowadays, of course, we sit side by side or face-to-face (or even screen to screen), not at anyone's feet, but the process remains the same. Awakening may not occur at the moment of hearing the pointer but rather gestate in the heart of the student and take birth there.

Here are three Advaita pointers from my years with Jean that had a powerful impact on me and "carry the perfume of their source." Essentially, each is a version of the fundamental self-inquiry question, "Who or what am I?" They invite us to take the backward step and turn our awareness back upon itself to discover the source of awareness itself.

- Throughout your life, from early childhood until now, you've used the word "I" as if you were referring to something continuous and unchanging. I did this, I saw that, I experienced this, I know that, I am this. But of course, all the cells in your body have died and been replaced multiple times. Your ideas and beliefs have changed and evolved, you've learned new things, taken on new roles, had different experiences.

Everything about you has changed, yet you continue to use the word "I." To what then does this word refer? Who or what is this that does not change even in the midst of constant change?

- Everything that you experience is an object of your experience: a table, a tree, a pet, a friend. If you're spiritually inclined, you might say that these objects are empty of substantiality or merely expressions of consciousness. Still, they're the objects of your experience, and for every object there must be a subject, for every experience an experiencer, to make the experience possible. But if you look for the subject or experiencer, you won't find it, because as soon as you do, it immediately becomes an object or an experience itself and loses its subjectivity. Can you find the experiencer prior to all experience, the ultimate subject of all objects?
- If you are the knower of your experience, you can't be the known. Both Jean Klein and Nisargadatta Maharaj taught that, in order to know what you are, it's helpful to become familiar with what you're not but have taken yourself to be: thoughts, emotions, personal history, self-image, body, senses, mind. If you're not any of these familiar ingredients of identity, then what are you really?

Some people find these pointers abstract, but if engaged wholeheartedly they invite a deep experiential inquiry into the nature of reality. They point beyond the mind by engaging the mind to help deconstruct what the mind thinks it knows.

Consider also these powerful short pointers attributed to three of the most prominent Advaita teachers of the last hundred years.

From Jean Klein (1912–98), a German-French teacher who studied Advaita in India after World War II and taught in Europe and the United States:

The seeker is the sought. The looker is what he or she is looking for.
In your absence is your presence.
Consciousness is the light behind all perceptions.
Everything that is, is consciousness.
Consciousness knows itself by itself; it is its own knowing.

From Nisargadatta Maharaj (1897–1981), an Indian teacher of Advaita from a tantric Hindu lineage who taught seekers from around the world in his small apartment in Mumbai:

Realization is not a new experience, it's the discovery of the timeless in every experience.
The door that locks you in is also the door that lets you out. The "I am" is the door. Stay at it until it opens.
All you have to do is find your source and take up your headquarters there.
Treating everything as a dream liberates.
Abandon false ideas, that's all. There's no need for true ideas. There aren't any.
You haven't understood until you've solved the riddle of the one who thinks they understand.

From Ramana Maharshi (1879–1950), the sage of Arunachala, whose ashram in southern India drew many thousands of seekers to sit in silent *darshan* or listen to his answers to the questions of devotees:

The one who thinks they're the doer is also the sufferer.
Immerse yourself in the living present. The future will take care of itself.
Transcend what and by whom? You alone exist.
The ever-present Self needs no efforts to be realized. Realization is already there. Illusion alone is to be removed.
To whom does all this appear?
Let what comes come. Let what goes go. Find out what remains.

Dzogchen-Mahamudra Pointers

In the Dzogchen tradition, the awakening journey begins with "pointing-out instructions" in which the teacher guides the student to recognize for themselves their natural state of inherent wakefulness. Known as the nature of mind, this wakefulness is the pure essence, basis, or foundation of the ordinary conceptual mind. Once this recognition has occurred and the teacher has verified its accuracy, the student spends time clarifying and deepening it and applying it to the challenges of everyday life until what often began as just a glimpse ripens into an abiding realization. (For more on pointing-out instructions, see "The Three Points of Garab Dorje" in chapter 2.)

In Dzogchen, the natural state of inherent wakefulness, known as rigpa, is understood to be a boundaryless, nonlocatable openness that is essentially empty, spontaneously knowing and aware, and inherently compassionate. It's often likened to a sunlit space, in which all experience arises in the limitless sunshine of awake awareness. Once recognized, the nature of mind does not evolve or change in any way. The ongoing practice, as in Advaita and Zen—where it's called "consciousness," "true self," or "buddha nature"—is to abide there and keep returning when you wander off.

Traditionally, you would need to engage in many years of intensive meditation and preliminary practices, including prostrations, visualizations, and mantra offerings, before you received pointing-out instructions from a qualified Dzogchen master. Today, certain teachers offer these instructions to students with far less preparation, or none at all, reasoning that most contemporary laypeople don't have the time or patience to invest years in preliminaries.

In addition to pointing-out instructions, the Mahamudra tradition, which is intimately linked both historically and philosophically with Dzogchen, offers a series of inquiry questions that gradually reveal, through direct experience, the inherently empty, awake, and dynamic nature of consciousness or mind. Often called "unfindability meditations," they invite the practitioner to locate and identify a variety of qualities or characteristics of mind that prove to be unfindable, which thereby releases the thinking mind from its obsessive search for finding an illusory ground in the manifest world. (For an example of a Mahamudra-style unfindability meditation, see "Investigating Your Thoughts" on page 145.)

Whether it's called buddha nature, consciousness, or the nature of mind, the three primary nondual traditions are clearly pointing to the same source, the same groundless ground, the same nonlocatable openness that encompasses all arising and remains unchanged and undisturbed. The terminology, pointers, cultural context, and methodology may differ, but there can only be a single moon, the pearl beyond price, the One without a second, to which these different fingers point. And, in the words of the Upanishads, you are That!

Practicing Presence

The simple practice of resting in awareness and allowing experience to be as it is has extraordinary awakening power. The inner spaciousness it offers for sensations, thoughts, and feelings to arise and pass away without the usual judgment or resistance emulates the selfless, boundaryless openness of our natural state of nondual presence and invites us to recognize and join it directly for ourselves. At the same time, we have an opportunity to get acquainted with the narratives, identities, and beliefs that keep arising in awareness and constitute the illusion of the separate self we take ourselves to be, so we don't keep getting seduced by them. (See the meditation "Effortless Mindfulness—Rest and Allow" on page 94.)

In our digitally distracted world, where most experiences are now mediated by a screen or other electronic interface, and facts have been reduced to hearsay rather than reliable evidence, being present for our direct experience has become both increasingly difficult and increasingly essential. One of the keys to the awakening process is the ability to welcome our experiences, both inner and outer. In direct, unmediated welcoming, we can eliminate the judging, interpreting mind and come into direct contact with nondual reality, prior to the illusory separation of subject and object. (For more on the importance of welcoming, see chapter 7.)

When I began studying with Jean Klein after many years of practicing zazen, I was inspired by his recommendation not to make a habit of meditation but to practice it only for the purpose of discovering the meditator. Faithfully following this guidance led to my own awakening. As a teacher myself, however, I've found that many people who don't have extensive experience with meditation could benefit from regular time spent being aware of thoughts and feelings as they arise and pass away—becoming aware, as Jean put it, of what we're not. As a follower of the direct approach, you can practice presence regularly not to achieve some distant goal promised by a progressive path, but as a direct invitation to drop the separate meditator and merge with nondual presence.

The great twentieth-century Tibetan Buddhist master Chögyam Trungpa advised practitioners to "develop a complete acceptance and openness" to all situations and emotions and to experience "everything totally without mental reservations and blockages." While meditating, he continued, you should "open yourself to the whole universe with absolute simplicity and nakedness of mind, letting go of all protecting barriers."[6] According to the contemporary Dzogchen teacher Yongey Mingyur Rinpoche, the fundamental approach is known as nonmeditation, nondistraction. That is, don't meditate in a concentrated effort to fabricate some special state, like happiness, clarity, or bliss, but at the same time stay present and aware of what's happening and follow the natural flow of the mind.[7]

In Zen, practicing presence in this way, without effort or end-gaining, is known as *shikantaza*, just sitting. Here's a description from the American Zen teacher Joan Halifax:[8]

> Zazen (*shikantaza*) is not meditation. It is not a mental exercise, a thing you do with your mind. It is not focused on practices that are antidotes to afflictive states or secondary consciousness. It is not about attaining a special state, being relaxed, or solving your problems. It is not about reducing stress, working with trauma, and being happy. Nor is it associated with visualizations or phrases to nurture certain qualities of mind.
>
> Zazen is about being radically open to things just as they are, not grasping at or rejecting phenomena, but simply being present and at ease with moment-to-moment uncertainty and groundlessness. It is fully embodied presence, with no separation between the mind, heart, body, and the context of our lived experience, and letting openness or not knowing deconstruct our version of reality. It is the method of non-method. Nothing extra, nothing added. This is zazen . . . just sitting upright.

Self-Inquiry

In the West, self-inquiry is often associated with the great Indian sage Ramana Maharshi, who recommended the practice of *atma-vichara* (literally, "self-deliberation" or "self-investigation") to many, though not all, of his students. Ramana assigned different practices, depending on the inclinations and maturity of the seekers who came to him, and atma vichara was probably the most popular. But atma vichara does not mean merely asking the question "Who am I?" over and over, as some people mistakenly assume.

According to David Godman, who has collected and translated Ramana's teachings, "Beginners in self-enquiry were advised by Sri Ramana to put their attention on the inner feeling of 'I' and to hold that feeling as long as possible. They would be told that if their attention was distracted by other thoughts they should revert to awareness of the 'I'-thought whenever they became aware that their attention had wandered." Ramana recommended various questions, such as 'Who am I?'

or "Where does this I come from?" whose ultimate aim was to make us continuously aware of the "I" that assumes it's responsible for all the activities of the body and the mind. Eventually the "I"-thought disappears and only an "effortless awareness of being" remains. "Self-enquiry should not be regarded as a meditation practice that takes place at certain hours and in certain positions," Godman continues, "it should continue throughout one's waking hours, irrespective of what one is doing. Sri Ramana Maharshi saw no conflict between working and self-enquiry, and he maintained that with a little practice it could be done under any circumstances."[9]

Of course, following the I-thought is just one form of self-inquiry. Contemplating the pointers of the teacher, as discussed in a previous section, naturally turns into a kind of self-inquiry as we reflect on them and endeavor to unlock the mystery of their meaning for ourselves. Essentially, self-inquiry involves turning our awareness away from the external objects on which it's habitually fixated back upon itself in an attempt to locate its source. The thirteenth-century Japanese Zen master Eihei Dogen called this "taking the backward step that turns the light of awareness inwardly to illuminate the [true] Self." The contents of experience are constantly changing, but that which is aware abides unchanging. Awareness is invited to become aware of itself as the ground of experience and the essence of what is.

Beginner's Mind Is Our Natural State

In the end, the point of the direct approach is not to gain more knowledge, but to return to a kind of primordial not-knowing, an openness prior to knowledge, a pure receptivity prior to any conclusion, or "no self" prior to any identification. This is the natural state we've been talking about, what the Zen master Suzuki Roshi called "beginner's mind" and equated with the Zen mind of the masters. "In the beginner's mind, there are many possibilities," he taught, "and in the expert's mind there are few."[10]

Someone once came to me for spiritual mentoring and professed to be a scientist who believed something to be true only if it met the criteria of the scientific method. "You mean," I asked, "that if you had an insight that you knew in your heart to be true without doubt, but it didn't meet the objective criteria of science, you wouldn't accept it?" "Yes, he said, I would need to prove it objectively." "Well," I responded, "then it's probably a waste of our time for us to work together."

In the monastery many years ago, I chose this koan from the *Book of Equanimity* (Shoyoroku) to contemplate and discuss during my tenure as head monk:

> Master Jizo asked the monk Hogen, "Where are you going?"
> Hogen said, "I'm wandering around aimlessly on pilgrimage."
> "What is the matter of your pilgrimage?" the master inquired.
> "I don't know," replied Hogen.
> "Not knowing is the most intimate," said Jizo.
> Hogen had a great awakening.

As this koan suggests, true intimacy with reality, or nondual presence, involves dropping the filters and concepts that separate us and resting in what the Korean Zen master Seung Sahn called "don't know mind." "Just go straight, don't know," he used to counsel his students.[11] Or as my teacher Jean Klein advised, live in nonconclusion and savor the ungraspable and inscrutable mystery of what is. As a former intellectual with a head full of ideas, this seemed like just the right koan for me to investigate as head monk, and it continues to inspire and inform my teaching of the direct approach more than forty years later.

Reflect and Inquire

Reflect on your own awakening journey. How has it unfolded to this point? What combination of direct and progressive methods and approaches have you explored? Which have had the most resonance and proved to be the most helpful for you? Have you encountered some of the limitations of each approach?

Of the skillful means offered in the direct approach for making yourself "awakening prone"—resting in awareness, self-inquiry, contemplating the pointers, connecting with sangha, direct contact with a teacher—which have you found most helpful? Which of the traditions has most appealed to you? If you switched from the progressive path to a more direct approach, what prompted you to do so? And how have you found the shift beneficial?

Q&A

Q: You emphasize the difference between the direct and progressive approaches, but the direct approach seems quite progressive in its way. For example, you recommend a variety of practices like effortless mindfulness and self-inquiry to elicit an awakening, and you talk in a previous chapter about how awakenings unfold and deepen over time. Isn't this a kind of progression? Otherwise, awakening would be instantaneous and complete.

A: From the perspective of the progressive approach, you need to practice constantly, according to certain established guidelines, to cultivate qualities and mind states that you don't already have to bring about an experience of awakening that's fundamentally different from the other experiences you've had. It's a kind of self-improvement project.

In the direct approach, you may use practices like self-inquiry, contemplation, or resting in awareness not to achieve some new and special state, but to point you back to qualities and capacities you already have, like your natural state of inherent wakefulness or your innate compassion. Inevitably, of course, awakening is a process that unfolds through time, but it's more a matter of becoming more fully who you always already are than becoming someone you're not. It's a homecoming, after years of wandering in search of home.

Q: In this chapter you talk about the practices of contemplation, meditation, and inquiry. How are they different, and what do you consider the benefits of each?

A: In the broadest sense, they're all forms of meditation—that is, ways of directing attention and awareness for spiritual purposes. Contemplation involves sitting with and reflecting on the teachings and pointers you read or listen to and allowing them to elicit a response inside you, generally an insight of some kind or a question that takes you deeper. If you read a passage that has special resonance, come back to it from time to time and contemplate its deeper meaning, beyond the words.

Meditation takes many forms, but the one I emphasize is simply resting in awareness and allowing everything to be as it is, offered here. As for inquiry, it comes in two forms: questions that point the mind back upon itself to discover the one who is aware (see the self-inquiry section in this chapter), and what I call deconstructive inquiry, questions that challenge the ideas, beliefs, identities, and stories that constitute the dream you inhabit. (For an example of deconstructive inquiry, see the meditation "Investigating Your Thoughts" on page 145.)

Meditation: Effortless Mindfulness–Rest and Allow

Take a few minutes to sit comfortably and shift your attention from your thinking to the coming and going of your breath. Allow your body and mind to settle.

Now, instead of practicing your regular meditation technique, sit quietly and let everything be the way it is. Don't focus or manipulate your attention in any way. Don't follow your breath. Don't do anything in particular. Just be fully present and let everything be–without trying to change or avoid or get rid of anything.

The fact is, your mind has no idea how to do this. It doesn't know how to let go. It only knows how to focus and hold on. But beyond the mind, there's a dimension of experience where letting go has already happened. This is your natural state of openness and receptivity.

At first, you may find these instructions baffling or confusing because we're so accustomed to working with our attention. In meditation, as in life, we're adept at doing but unfamiliar with nondoing.

When I say just let everything be the way it is, your mind takes it as an injunction to do something special. Instead, consider it an invitation to rest in the openness that's always already taking place.

Consider the sky, for example. It doesn't have to do anything to include the birds, the planes, the clouds, and the other objects that pass through it. By nature, the sky is open and all-inclusive. The same is true of your natural state of inherent wakefulness. Any effort to practice openness just takes you away from the innate openness of your natural state.

Most of the time your attention is focused on objects, whether they're internal, like thoughts, feelings, or sensations, or external, like material things, and you interpret them to create an inner world of meaning that has little to do with the way things actually are. Instead, let go of this contraction around objects. Let go of the tendency to judge and interpret, and just relax back into awareness itself.

Rest as the open, unconditional awareness in which experiences come and go. The operative word here is rest. No doing, no manipulation, no end-gaining. This awareness is inherently silent, inherently present, inherently still; it doesn't do anything. It simply welcomes what is, just the way it is. Let yourself rest as this silent, open, unconditional awareness or presence for as long as you like.

No need to constantly check to make sure you're doing it right. Just rest as awareness. Let go of all doing, and let everything be as it is, inside and outside.

When you notice that your attention is no longer open and has become fixated on objects again, gently return to rest as awareness, and let everything be as it is. Continue to rest and allow for as long as you like, then go about your day.

5

Why Bother with a Teacher?

Some people wake up to their nondual spiritual nature suddenly and unexpectedly. While walking in the woods, reading a book, talking with a friend, listening to a piece of music, or sitting quietly on their meditation cushion, their usual way of perceiving reality drops away, awareness expands, the sense of self dissolves, the gap between self and other, inside and outside, collapses, and a completely new way of being reveals itself—much to their amazement and surprise.

Others, in their attempts to alleviate their suffering or satisfy their curiosity, turn to spiritual texts and teachings for guidance and follow well-established practices for achieving the enlightenment they've read about in books. After years of regular application, they may have a glimpse of what they're looking for—or much, much more. But in the end, sudden or gradual, deep or shallow, just about every seeker finds themselves in relationship with a teacher.

In my own case, teachers played a major role in my unfolding. Provocative stories of the masters of old piqued my interest, baffled my mind, and led me inexorably to a zendo to begin formal Zen practice. Photos and stories of a particular teacher drew me on a cross-country quest that culminated in becoming a monk and practicing for years under his guidance and the guidance of others in his tradition.

In my years as a monk and after, I had the opportunity to spend time with some extraordinary teachers from a variety of spiritual traditions. Simply being in the presence of certain teachers had a profound and lasting impact on me, even if I never studied with them formally. Teachers have inspired me, guided me, educated me, disillusioned me (in several senses), disappointed me, awakened me, and ultimately invited me to become a teacher myself.

My journey has revolved and evolved around teachers, and I feel the utmost gratitude and appreciation for their presence in my life. As a result, I recommend to many if not most of the people who come to me for spiritual guidance that they ultimately settle on a teacher to engage with over an extended period of time, whether before or after having an awakening themselves.

At the same time, the introduction of Eastern spiritual teachings and practices to the West has been littered with collateral damage from teachers—both Eastern and Western—who have acted in insensitive, unskillful, and downright abusive ways. As a student myself I witnessed such behavior on the part of several teachers and saw the negative impact it had on their students. And as a journalist I've written about its effect not only on students but on the teachings themselves, as practitioners have turned their back on the Dharma and the beneficial practices they engaged in for years because of the understandable doubts and distrust this behavior evoked.

The teacher-student relationship is often a powerful one, driven by love and dedication and a desire to end suffering, fraught with often unrealistic ideas and expectations, and eliciting some of the most primal needs and urges on both sides—and for these reasons it's prone to some egregious forms of acting out. In this chapter, we'll explore in detail the teacher-student relationship and the benefits and pitfalls of studying with a teacher.

Role of the Teacher in the Direct Approach

Teachers traditionally play a crucial role in the direct approach to spiritual awakening, offering the "special transmission outside the scriptures"[1] that the founder of Zen in China, Bodhidharma, recommends. In the Vedanata tradition of India, the presence of a teacher (*darshan*) is considered a key element in the awakening process, and in Tibetan Dzogchen pointing-out instructions from a qualified teacher are considered the necessary first step in realizing the nature of mind.

Teachers embody and exemplify the awakened condition for their students and act as an inspiration on the path. In the absence of a living teacher, awakening can seem like a distant prospect that only the great sages of other times and places have experienced. Being in the presence of someone who lives an awakened life shows that awakening is possible in this lifetime and brings our own inherent wakefulness to the foreground. Indeed, the presence of the teacher alone is sometimes sufficient to catalyze an awakening.

Just to be clear, the teacher does not provide you with something you don't already have. Quite the contrary, they point your awareness back upon what you always already are: consciousness, true nature, awakened awareness, your natural state of nondual presence. But at the right moment this pointing can be sufficient to initiate a powerful shift in the locus of your identity (see chapter 3, page 47).

Rather than give extensive talks, Advaita teachers like Nisargadatta Maharaj and Jean Klein preferred to meet with groups of students in dialogue, inviting questions and responding directly with pointers from the depths of their understanding. Such gatherings are traditionally known as *satsang* (literally, "being together in truth"). Jean's responses were often followed by long silences in which students steeped in his wisdom and the quality of his presence and allowed it to permeate our being and point us to our already awake true nature. I often found the silences far more profound than the words.

Judging from the videos and the reports of people who visited him in Mumbai, gatherings with Nisargadatta could be quite animated and, occasionally, especially in his later years, he could get visibly angry when he thought students lacked sincerity and dedication. Though no doubt difficult to hear, I'm sure his exhortations had a galvanizing effect. As one American spiritual teacher put it, dead gurus don't kick ass, but living teachers whose entire lives are devoted to conveying the truth may give their students a forceful nudge in the right direction from time to time.

A Note on the Term "Teacher"

In English we tend to use the term "teacher" quite broadly to apply to a range of different roles and functions. For example, an instructor is a teacher who offers basic teachings and methodologies without claiming any deeper wisdom; a *pandit* or *geshe* is often a scholar with academic training and expertise in certain areas of knowledge; the sage is a wise being who may or may not actively teach but leads by his example; and the guru is generally an awakened being who epitomizes the teachings and is held up as an object of veneration and sometimes even worship. The teacher in the direct approach may encompass some or all these different functions at various times, depending on their inclination and tradition.

Pointer: The Map Is Not the Territory

When I teach the School for Awakening, I generally end by expressing my hope that people leave knowing less than when they came. All knowledge is a form of ignorance, taught the great Indian sage Nisargadatta Maharaj. The most accurate map is still just a map, not the territory, just an image and not reality. Don't become fixated on words and concepts and lose sight of the vibrant, mysterious, and inexpressible reality to which they merely point—and for which silence is ultimately the most accurate voice. In fact, my most fervent wish–and the wish of any true teacher –is that you'll forget everything I've said and fall off the edge of knowledge into the ineffable.

The Teacher-Student Relationship

In an apocryphal statement long attributed to Sigmund Freud, the founder of psychoanalysis is famously said to have complained that he couldn't treat one of his patients because she refused to fall in love with him. Putting aside the gender and power imbalances implied in this claim, Freud was suggesting that the healing power of the relationship depended on an attachment based on love, at least in one direction. For the patient to get better, she needed to love and idealize the therapist, in a process known as transference. (Subsequent therapists, including Freud himself no doubt, discovered that transferences could be both positive and negative, and analyzing the transference became a crucial part of the therapeutic process.)

In the same way, students of spirituality often idealize and fall in love with the teacher, projecting the best and highest qualities that in fact both people possess onto only one of the parties in the relationship. Such powerful transference has embedded within it the potential for enormous abuse. If the teacher believes the transference and becomes intoxicated and inflated as a result of being seen in this way, they may consciously or unconsciously use the power projected onto them to take advantage of the relationship and the student. By contrast, if the teacher recognizes the projection and refuses to identify with it—and instead reflects it back to the student as in fact belonging to them, as much as to the teacher—the relationship can be a potent vehicle for spiritual empowerment and awakening.

Jean Klein spoke about this process often and exemplified the refusal to identify with the projection in his own relationships with students. When I first met with him individually, I was astonished to realize—after years of working with teachers who soaked up my projections and used them to their own advantage—that he had no interest in my being his student. I could not feel the grasping and identification I had felt so often from teachers in the past. He often warned us to be aware of any teacher who "had students" and called his sangha simply "friends of Jean Klein."

Invariably Jean would point to the deepest level of the teacher-student relationship, in which the roles of teacher and student fall away in simply being. One person might play the part of teacher, like any other part in the play of life, but should not lay claim to or identify with it. From a more psychological perspective, we could say that an individual can embody the guru principle or archetype for others from time to time, but ultimately it doesn't belong to them. If they claim it as their possession, they run the risk of becoming inflated and misusing the power the archetype confers.

In practice, however, the archetype is deliberately invoked in some traditions to impress upon the student the power of the teachings and bind student to teacher in the transformative process of spiritual awakening, a process that can be quite intense and require a deep level of confidence and trust. In Tibetan Buddhism the student visualizes and prays to the teacher as the embodiment of the guru archetype, on the same level as the deities the student invokes as well. In Zen, the roshi is revered as an awakened being who safeguards secret teachings that the student aspires to realize for themselves. As I mentioned earlier, this approach creates the potential for misunderstanding and abuse, as we've witnessed on numerous occasions here in the West. In other traditions, including Advaita and Buddhist vipassana, the teacher is usually regarded as more of a "spiritual friend" *(kalyana mitra)*—that is, just another human being like the student but further along on the path.

How Teachers Go Astray

I first became aware of the numerous ways a spiritual teacher can misuse their power when the Zen master I'd been studying with turned out to be an alcoholic who was propositioning women in the interview room and having an extramarital affair with his principal female disciple. Since then, I've watched a series of teachers take advantage of their position and leave confused and disillusioned students in their wake. Some have acted unconsciously and expressed deep remorse when the effects of their behavior were brought to their attention. Others have acted deliberately and relentlessly, despite being confronted repeatedly about the damage they were causing.

For example, one well-known teacher who espoused the view that doing just happens but there is no doer, when confronted by female students about his sexual advances, explained that he wasn't in charge of his actions and so couldn't be held accountable. Another, using what I like to call Advaita logic, insisted that the anger he directed toward students who didn't do what he told them to was just illusory and couldn't possibly be a problem, even though it clearly caused suffering for others. If everything is perfect as it is, these teachers argue, then no behavior or emotion is unacceptable. Although this may be true on what is called the absolute or ultimate level, on the relative level of personal relationships and real-world functioning, there are clear-cut and widely accepted boundaries and guidelines around what's kind and acceptable that we universally agree upon as appropriate.

Fortunately, there are also excellent, ethical, wise, and compassionate teachers in the nondual tradition. But the question of how and why people who have apparently dedicated their lives to realizing the nondual nature of reality and their intimate interconnectedness with all of life could abuse their power and take advantage of others deserves special attention. It's not an easy question to answer, and I certainly can't do it justice here, though I have written about it extensively in other places.[2]

The short and most generous answer is that even the most awakened among us are imperfect and will occasionally stumble and act out our more primitive and conditioned impulses. Even though we may know we're not a separate self but an inextricable part of a web of life that is itself our deepest nature, we still act, often or just at times, from a more limited and self-serving worldview. As students, we need to be aware of this inevitable imperfection (in the midst of the innate perfection) and proceed with caution in working with a teacher.

The long answer includes a number of factors and forces that deserve brief mention. The first is what my friend John Welwood calls "spiritual bypassing."[3] Essentially, spiritual bypassing happens when the person who awakens to the timeless, transcendent nature of reality makes no effort to face and transform old reactive patterns and self-serving behaviors in the light of this new understanding but instead ignores them and pretends to hang out in the transcendent. Often these patterns are based on a lifetime of conditioning and not easily recognizable, and there may be tremendous resistance to dealing with them as well. In psychological circles, these are known as shadow elements and may require years of investigation and self-inquiry to recognize and release. When the teacher has a history of trauma, the split between the conscious mind and visible persona and the forces at work in the shadows can be especially pronounced. Each of us who awakens is called upon to integrate this awakening into our lives by addressing the issue of spiritual bypassing, as I discuss in the later chapters of this book. But the imperative is especially pronounced for teachers, who have such a powerful influence on the spiritual lives of their students.

The second factor is narcissism and its more virulent cousin, sociopathy. Narcissism exists on a spectrum, from so-called normal narcissism—that is, self-serving behavior that normal people with egos engage in—to pathological narcissism, characterized by an exaggerated sense of self-importance, a belief in one's own entitlement, limited or no empathy, and the exploitation of others. Pathological narcissism can be difficult to spot because it's often hidden beneath a veneer of charm and charisma and at least the appearance of sincerity and dedication to the well-being of others. For obvious reasons, narcissists are naturally drawn to positions that attract the kind of admiration they crave, and what more fitting position than guru, expert, or spiritual teacher? Sociopathy adds to narcissism a pathological disregard for the feelings or needs of others and a repudiation of social norms and legal constraints.

From my experience, both directly as a student and from a distance as a journalist and a psychotherapist, I would say that most of the teachers who have acted abusively and taken advantage of their students have been driven by their narcissistic need for admiration and self-aggrandizement. One Zen master I studied with for almost five years demeaned his students publicly, bragged about his accomplishments, had grandiose plans for expanding the community to reflect his importance, and consistently blamed others for his shortcomings. Yet he was charming and charismatic and through his belief in his own specialness made those who studied with him feel special as well.

Fortunately, gaslighting and the other insidious ploys of narcissists have gained widespread notoriety in recent years, and we can hope that in the aftermath of the Me Too movement the abuse of women in particular is no longer as easy as it once was. Nevertheless, I recommend watching for the telltale signs of narcissism in prospective teachers and checking them out thoroughly.

Can genuinely awakened teachers still act narcissistically on a consistent basis? Clearly, narcissism and the nondual perspective that there is no separate self to serve and we're inextricably connected with all of life would seem to be antithetical. Most narcissistic teachers are probably in fact imposters—or at best only halfway up the mountain or stuck in spiritual bypassing—with no fully awakened understanding to share. But given the extraordinary complexity of the human heart and psyche, there do appear to be people who teach in whom both narcissism and awakening coexist. Best to keep your eyes wide open and trust your inner knowing.

Take the Time to Check Out a Teacher

The Dalai Lama counsels prospective students to spend several years checking out a Buddhist teacher to make sure they walk their talk and live according to the teachings they espouse before committing to work with them. In the Tibetan tradition, teachers often function as gurus and become an object of their students' devotion, and once accepted by a guru the student is expected to take a vow of allegiance that can only be broken with severe karmic consequences.

Today in the West, especially in the case of teachers who have no established lineage or tradition, students may study with a number of teachers without pledging any allegiance or even having any direct interpersonal contact. As a result, the same caveats don't necessarily apply. But the teacher-student relationship can be complex, especially when strong feelings and attachments are involved, and if you find yourself drawn to a particular teacher, for the very good reasons I enumerated earlier in this chapter, I recommend spending at least some time checking them out as the Dalai Lama advises.

Based on my own years of study and practice, my experience with teachers, and the reports I've received from seekers over the years, I've put together a list of the qualities I believe a true teacher will possess. In the Zen tradition the precepts that guide ethical behavior are considered, at the deepest level, to be descriptions of how an enlightened person would naturally act. By nature, an awakened teacher who does not see others as separate from themselves would not kill, steal, lie, or exploit their students for their own benefit. In this spirit, I offer the guidelines for teacher integrity not as a list of shoulds and should nots but as descriptions of how a true teacher behaves. Most teachers will not be able to live up to this ideal completely, but you have every right to expect a close approximation:

- The true teacher doesn't need anything from you, including your love, admiration, veneration, power, or money.
- They do not require your loyalty or allegiance to anything but the truth of your being as you understand it.
- Their primary purpose is to further your spiritual unfolding, not to build their organization or expand their popularity on social media.

- The teacher does not attempt to organize, orchestrate, or control your personal life and does not purport to know what's best for you on a personal level.
- The true teacher welcomes honest feedback, acknowledges their imperfect humanness, and takes responsibility for their mistakes rather than defending themselves and blaming others.
- They don't take themselves to be a teacher and don't take you to be a student, except as temporary roles in the dance of life. In the absence of any projection, you're free to realize who you really are.
- The guru is an archetype or energy, not an individual person. Be careful about projecting this archetype onto a fallible human being, it's a setup for disillusionment and exploitation.
- The true teacher doesn't take themselves to be a guru but points instead to the true guru inside you.
- The true teacher is aware of the tendency among seekers to idealize their teachers and project their own assumptions and expectations upon them. Knowing this, the teacher doesn't (mis)use these projections for their own personal gain and aggrandizement.
- The teacher realizes that the term "enlightened person" is an oxymoron and does not claim this identity. In the presence of enlightenment, the ego is absent and there's no one to claim it.
- The teacher is merely the finger pointing at the radiant moon of your true nature. Once you've glimpsed the moon, you needn't focus on the finger.
- The realization "I am That" reveals that there is only That, not that there is only me. The first is called awakening; the second is called narcissism.

- The teacher has a responsibility to be impeccable in their dealings with students because they represent a world of meaning that the student reveres and aspires to understand.
- The true teacher, the one who dedicates their life to the awakening of others, naturally elicits our gratitude and respect and does not need to demand it.

Like the Dalai Lama, I recommend spending time getting to know a teacher at close range—admittedly difficult to do in this post-Covid era when most gatherings occur online—and checking them out thoroughly. How do they treat their students? Are they patient and compassionate, or prone to be pushy and demanding? Are they humble or inflated? Do they expect subservience? Do they treat their students as equals? How do their students behave? If you can't spend time with the teacher, feel free to ask probing and uncomfortable questions of their students. I studied with a Tibetan teacher for several years but left when I began noticing how poorly he treated the female students who worked tirelessly on his behalf. Years later I learned that he was forcing these students to have sex with him and was eventually repudiated by the Dalai Lama himself.

Of course, at the deepest level everything happens as it must in the mysterious scheme of things. As one Zen master put it, there is no right or wrong—yet right is right and wrong is wrong. In other words, there are no absolute standards, everything is innately perfect and complete as it is. Yet on the relative level everything is not simply subjective, we have an intuitive and heartfelt sense of right and wrong that we share as human beings across cultures and informs how we act.

At the absolute level, whatever happens is what was meant to happen in the mystery of this human manifestation. At the same time someone who purports to guide others has a responsibility to lead a life in alignment with truth. Both are true, and we can't be excusing abusive behavior, as teachers like the one I mentioned earlier have done, by claiming that everything is just happening in the absence of a doer. Yes, no doer, nothing done, no self, no other—now in the world of apparent time and space apply this understanding to your interactions with others and act from your deepest inner knowing. Otherwise, step back from teaching and take stock of your life.

As students, we have a responsibility to pay attention, use discernment, and resist the temptation to give our power away. But we bring our vulnerability, confusion, and unresolved psychological issues with us on the spiritual path, and the teacher, by virtue of their role as a guide and exemplar, must be committed to being as impeccable as humanly possible. This means doing the nitty-gritty post-awakening work of allowing the truth they've realized to penetrate the dark corners of their life and turn them to the ruthless, compassionate scrutiny of the light. If you're not willing to do the work or think you don't have dark corners, please don't put yourself forward as a teacher.

Advice to Students in Their Relationships with Teachers

As students of inevitably imperfect teachers, we have a responsibility to ourselves to act wisely, trust our deeper knowing, set clear boundaries, and take care of ourselves.

- Remember, you are the path and no one else is an expert on you. The teacher's job may be to offer powerful pointers to your essential nature and to challenge and expand your limited view of reality. But in the end only you can know what's right for you to study or practice; only you, in the crucible of your own heart, can forge a deeper understanding. Develop a keen inner radar, an intuitive gut knowing that guides your life, and trust it. The true guru is inside you!
- Never give up your own inner authority and autonomy; surrender to life, not to another person, even if they claim to be

an authority on you. For those of us tired of making difficult decisions and navigating our way through this complex world, it can be appealing to consider ceding authority and responsibility to someone else. But each of us expresses the one essential nature we share in our own inimitable way; we have a unique trajectory, purpose, and set of gifts to offer, and we betray this unique contribution when we give up our autonomy and let someone else tell us how to run our life. You can never say yes wholeheartedly unless you feel you have the right to say no.

- Love your messy human incarnation, and recognize that you have an innate value, just by being you, that doesn't require you to be good or special or depend on the reflected stature of a teacher. If you have underlying feelings of inadequacy, as so many of us do, face them directly, see them for what they are, and release their hold over you. This is not easy to do, but it's essential if you're going to resist the pull to get validation from teachers. One of the most direct ways to release inadequacy is to wake up to your true nature, which is inherently perfect and pure, beyond good and bad, right and wrong, adequate and inadequate.
- If you feel you've been exploited or abused by a teacher, turn first to other members of the sangha to express your concerns and find out if any of them have had similar experiences. Together you will have more power to confront the teacher, if necessary, and seek outside support. Some spiritual communities have ethical guidelines and processes you can follow if the teacher has violated them. In most cases, however, communities tend to be slow to disturb the status quo or question established authority, though this pattern may finally be changing in the Me Too era.
- Consider that, as both Being itself—limitless, inviolable, and undisturbed—and separate individual beings, with our unique

> talents, conditioning, and genetic endowment, we're called upon to navigate a twofold journey: waking up to the deepest truth of our being and becoming mature human beings with the capacity to love and work. If we focus on psychological maturity alone, we may always feel we haven't plumbed the mystery and realized the happiness and peace that come from discovering the deeper meaning and purpose of life. But if we focus only on realizing the absolute and never grow up to express our potential as human beings, we fail to do the essential work of embodying spirit in the world of form.

Transmission and Lineage

Transmission between teacher and student occurs constantly as you receive and resonate with the teachings and the presence of the teacher and allow them to ripen in the crucible of your own heart. The teacher conveys and elicits the awakening experience in their students through a combination of the skillful means at their disposal, but especially through the nondual presence in which they abide and which they inherently share with their students. Jean Klein used to say that true transmission happens in silence when the teacher who does not take themselves to be a teacher meets the student who does not take themselves to be a student. In this timeless moment, free of roles, hierarchies, and limited identities, a mutual recognition and acknowledgment takes place.

Jean never formally appointed anyone as his successor or gave what might be called formal transmission, believing no doubt that genuine transmission is not something one person can confer upon another. In the Zen tradition, by contrast, transmission takes the form of a ceremony acknowledging the passing of the Dharma from "one warm hand to another," as my first Zen teacher put it, and conferring on the disciple the authority to teach. The lineage of teachers who have transmitted the Dharma down through the centuries and preserved its purity and integrity is revered in Zen and often recited in the monastery, and disciples in a particular lineage are taught to call upon their deceased predecessors for support and guidance in their own practice and teaching.

As examples I offer the poems my Zen teacher and I exchanged to acknowledge and celebrate the Dharma transmission that took place in silence between us. In lieu of a formal ceremony, we had tea together and exchanged gifts: I gave him a book by Nyogen Senzaki, the Japanese teacher who first brought Zen to America, signed by the author, and he gave me his *oryoki*, the nested bowls used for eating in the zendo during retreat. Afterward, we visited his teacher, who lived nearby, and received her blessings. As you can see, the poems acknowledge the personal teacher-student relationship as well as the ineffable relationship of one mind and one heart to itself that finds expression in the mutual acknowledgment of transmission.

Transmission Poem from Stephan to Adyashanti:

Nothing to teach,
yet teaching happens.
Nothing to transmit,
yet transmission has already occurred.

Just one mind in every direction
as far as the eye can see
constantly dancing
in a myriad of forms.

The gateless gate: When this mind
recognizes itself from one warm hand
to another, nothing changes,
yet the gratitude is inexhaustible!

—Stephan (Dharma Ocean, Pure Practice)

Transmission Poem from Adyashanti to Stephan:

Everything ends where it began
in intimate friendship.

Clear sky to clouds
clouds to rain
rain to rivers
rivers to mountains
mountains to rivers
rivers to rain
rain to clouds
clouds to clear sky.

Not one step has been taken
and yet walking continues.

The Buddhist journey ends in being Buddha.
I happily sing your name to the stars
as infinite Buddha eyes bear witness to
the birth of great realization.

Nothing has happened
finally.

And yet this heart warms
to the hand-to-hand
touch being received.

Each time it happens
this life completes itself
again.

With Great Love and Tenderness,

—Adya (Silent Wind)

Lineage endeavors to keep the truth alive in the human realm and purports to guarantee an accuracy and vitality that can get lost over the centuries if the teachings are diluted or distorted, as they are in so many spiritual traditions. The process of formal transmission can be a kind of vetting process leading to an official seal of approval, a kind of certification that this person is worthy of trust. For the disciple, transmission may be both empowering and humbling because it reminds them that they are just one representative of a time-honored tradition.

Unfortunately, this process is as imperfect and unreliable as the people who engage in it, and most of the Zen teachers who have taken advantage of their students over the years have received official transmission. In the end, choosing the right teacher is a purely intuitive and individual process, subject to the same inner knowing as following the pathless path. For myself, I have the utmost gratitude for my teachers and feel that I'm merely passing along in my limited way the profound wisdom that was so generously and selflessly transmitted to me.

Reflect and Inquire

Spend some time reflecting on your experiences with teachers over the years. Have you had teachers in school or other endeavors like work or sports who had a major positive impact on your life? What have you learned from them that you might not have learned on your own? Or has your contact with teachers been largely disappointing, conflictual, or even exploitative or abusive? How about spiritual teachers? Have you witnessed or heard about some of the negative behaviors discussed in this chapter? How has it impacted your life and colored your view of the role of teacher?

In the realm of awakening, what qualities seem to draw you to certain teachers? Is it primarily the directness and accessibility of their teachings? Or is it their charisma, the air of authority, the gentleness and compassion, the genuineness and responsiveness? What do you imagine you can get from a teacher that you don't already have on your own? One teacher once put his hand on my heart and said the true guru is inside you, then turned out to be a charlatan who exploited and abused his students. What standards do you think a spiritual teacher should live up to?

Reflect on the many qualities you expect from a teacher of awakening and wonder whether they may in fact be qualities you already possess. If they are, how could you access them directly from your own heart and mind rather than through another person? And how could you access the gifts the teacher alone provides without forsaking your own innate wisdom and giving your power away?

Q&A

Q: As you describe it, the teacher-student relationship seems quite complicated and rife with the potential for confusion and abuse. I'm not sure why I would want to engage with a teacher in this way. Wouldn't it just be easier to stick with my books, podcasts, and videos?

A: The true teacher embodies the awakened understanding they teach. They're committed to living from the truth of their being moment after moment. As a result, spending time in their presence points you back again and again to the awakened perspective that's always already available inside your own heart and mind. This vital and direct transmission beyond words can only be found in the presence of a teacher, even if it's merely online. Of course, nowadays it's difficult to find a teacher who's available for contact on a regular basis, so the point may be moot. But if you have an opportunity to hang out with someone who's committed to living an awakened life, whether or not they teach, I recommend taking it.

Q: You say that even after a genuine awakening old habitual patterns and impulses may arise that cause someone to behave in self-centered and even hurtful ways. How is it possible to experience self-centeredness if the very foundation for selfish behavior has dissolved? After all, when there is no identification with self, there is no possibility for selfish behavior.

A: In most awakenings, the recognition that there is no separate self doesn't eliminate all identification in one go, and old identities will continue to assert their influence. This is a natural and inevitable stage in the awakening process, and ongoing investigation and inquiry are required to free the person from the tenacious grip of the dream narrative with a me at the center (for more on deconstructing the dream, see chapter 6, page 119). But if a person latches on to the identity of being awakened, proclaims themselves to be a teacher prematurely, and refuses to do the ongoing investigation required to establish themselves in an abiding understanding of no self, self-centered behavior is not only possible but likely, with unfortunate consequences for all concerned.

Meditation: Is Anything Missing?

Begin by sitting comfortably for a few moments with your eyes open and gaze around the room. As you gaze, notice how your mind habitually judges and interprets what you see. "The furniture looks old and shabby," you may think. "That pile of papers is an eyesore. The carpet's stained. The bills need to be paid." Your mind is constantly making comments like these, adding a conceptual overlay that makes it difficult for you to experience reality directly.

Even concepts like "book" and "table" limit your ability to see beyond the form to the underlying essence of what is. This ongoing commentary leaves you feeling restless, dissatisfied, and endlessly yearning for a better life.

Now close your eyes for a few moments and then slowly open them again. This time gaze around you as if you were an extraterrestrial who's just landed on Earth, or an infant who's just been born. Look at the window, the computer, the table, the chair, with beginner's mind, as if you've never seen them before and have no idea what they are.

Enjoy the play of light and dark, color and form, movement and stillness, without giving names to the display. Allow yourself to abide in a natural state of openness and wonder. You have no idea what anything is, and your mind doesn't need to intervene between awareness and the experience arising in awareness. Notice how this innocent, open looking acts on your being. How does your relationship with your experience change?

After several minutes of innocent looking, gently ask yourself, "On present evidence only, without consulting the mind, is there anything missing or lacking in my experience right now?" Notice what happens.

If this question makes no sense to you, just let it go and continue your innocent looking. If your mind starts recounting a familiar story about what you apparently need but don't have, about how your life is lacking or inadequate in some way, set it aside and go back to simply looking. Remember, you've been asked to consult present evidence only.

Now ask the question again: "On present evidence only, without consulting the mind, is there anything missing or lacking in my experience right now?" Allow an answer to emerge. If you conclude that nothing is missing or lacking, notice how this realization changes your experience of what is. How does it feel to realize that nothing is missing or lacking right now? That everything is complete just the way it is? That no teacher or teaching is required to make things clearer or more fully what they already are?

If this isn't your conclusion, just return to innocent looking for a few more minutes and ask yourself the question one more time before getting up and going about your day.

6

Deconstructing the Dream

The great nondual wisdom traditions teach that each of us lives in a dream of our own devising, an imaginary realm with an illusory separate self at the center and an apparent world out there constructed of our ideas, beliefs, memories, self-images, stories, plans, fears, and aspirations. This dream is like a comfortable bubble that encloses us in its familiar embrace, and it's so complex and well-elaborated and seems to work so well most of the time that we rarely if ever recognize it or question it in any way. At the same time, it's the lens we're looking through, the filter that colors our perceptions and judgments and renders the way things actually are virtually invisible to us, hidden by a veil of projections and misconceptions.

Whether it's rich, expansive, and comfortably furnished, or impoverished, narrow, and stark, this dream world is based on a detailed narrative we've cobbled together over a lifetime of childhood experiences, early life education and conditioning, successes, traumas, disappointments, and the beliefs, ideas, and preferences we've picked up along the way. If we were shamed or abused as children, for example, this dream may cast us as inherently worthless and other people as out to hurt or reject us, unless we manage to have corrective experiences that contradict the narrative. If we were loved and protected as children and led adult lives of relative happiness and success, we may be convinced we have inherent value and expect others to love and value us as well.

Most of us, of course, have more complicated narratives that mix the positive and the negative, the hopeful and the fearful, the self-valuing and the self-critical. Indeed, we're constantly constructing and reconstructing the narrative, changing the viewpoints and interpretations as we go. One moment we're the hero of our life story, the next moment the victim; one moment the world is a loving, beneficent place filled with happiness and contentment, the next we're seemingly besieged by adversaries and problems we're struggling to overcome. But every narrative, every dream, no matter how static or unpredictable, simple or complex, posits a separate self at the center to which the narrative refers, and it's inevitably no more than a limited and lifeless imitation of reality that prevents the true, the authentic, the wondrous, the sublime, and the sacred from breaking through and revealing itself to us.

If you want to know your dream, consider how you talk about yourself and your views of life when others ask who you are—or what your mind is constantly telling you in the default-mode self-talk of the brain as you go about your day. This dream constitutes the world as we know it. We surround ourselves with it wherever we go and constantly consult it to tell us where we are, who we are, and where we're going. We set it aside like a suit of clothes when we drift off to sleep, replacing it perhaps with other dreams, but immediately put it back on when we get up in the morning lest we feel lost, disoriented, and out of sorts.

In fact, we're enthralled by our dream and resistant to waking up because we consider ourselves to be the dreamer and derive our meaning from the dream. The highs and lows, the sorrow and the exultation, provide the juice and emotional involvement that both motivate and torment us, and we're afraid to wake up because we don't know what our lives would be like without the familiar drama we take to be reality.

Once it dawns on us that we're living in a dream—as a result of meditation or psychotherapy or an uneasy sense that things aren't as they seem—we may devote ourselves to shoring up the dream and doing whatever we can to make it more comfortable or manageable by substituting more positive beliefs and stories for the ones we've believed until now. This concerted effort to construct a better dream is the province of the New Age and self-help movements. As the old metaphor goes, we're trying to rearrange the deck chairs on the *Titanic* and not entertaining the more radical proposition that the ship is no longer sustainable—or, even more deeply, that it's never been real or viable to begin with.

Living in such a claustrophobic world of concepts and illusions, one step removed from reality, no wonder so many of us, especially in these challenging times, lead lives filled with boredom, anxiety, depression, and addiction to distractions that temporarily substitute another more appealing dream for the one we find so stifling. In the end, nothing we tell ourselves about reality is true. It's inevitably a story or construct because reality eludes our every attempt to conceptualize and catch it. In words attributed to the Advaita sage Nisargadatta Maharaj, anything you think you are, you're not. The spiritual journey involves waking up from this narrative bubble into the vivid, vibrant, unpredictable, nondual reality of right now, free of an imagined future or a poorly remembered past, acknowledging our projections, memories, beliefs, and expectations but not believing or indulging them.

For many people, the journey of awakening begins with the recognition that the dream we inhabit is the cause of our dissatisfaction, and only by waking up from it and emerging into the light can we relieve this dissatisfaction once and for all. Once we recognize that we're merely a dream character in an illusory scenario created and perpetuated by the mind can we recognize and abide as our true nature beyond the mind. If we liken reality to a vast ocean of being, at once infinitely diverse and multifaceted and at the same time unified in its oneness as the limitless totality of what is, our individual dream narrative is merely a bubble among countless others, floating on the surface and trapped in believing itself to be the true reality. The only way to escape the confines of our bubble is to wake up to being the ocean.

Meditation: Getting to Know the Dream You Inhabit

Begin by sitting quietly and resting awareness on the breath for a few moments.

Consider your life as you currently live it. Who do you take yourself to be? What is your self-image? How do you define yourself? What stories do you repeatedly tell yourself and others—about life, about yourself, about other people? How do these stories distort reality and limit how you think and behave? What are the unique ways you filter what you see and hear and fail to see reality as it is? And how has this bubble caused you suffering by limiting your ability to connect with life directly?

As you go about your day, be aware of how the self-and-world construct keeps recreating and reinforcing itself in your inner dialogue, the repetitive thoughts that run through your mind. "These are the people and situations I need to manage or protect myself from," you may think. "These are my allies and adversaries, my advantages and disadvantages. These are my problems and possibilities." Notice how this construct causes you to react and interact with others. Are these habitual thoughts true? Are they an accurate representation of reality? Do they constitute your true identity, who you really are? Or are they just the mind chatter that is so enthralling and convincing and distracts you from recognizing the truth of who you are?

Let these questions be your practice for the next day or two. Return to them repeatedly throughout the day as you become more and more familiar with the bubble you perpetuate, your unique self-and-world construct.

Then ask yourself, when I use the ever-present word "I," aren't I referring to the one who is aware of the content, not the content itself? Aren't "I" really this context, this background, this deeper ground of awareness itself? Even the most intimate inner feelings and secret longings, the dreams and memories you hold to be so precious, are just more content in the limitless context, awakened awareness, that you really are. See them for what they are, rather than identifying with them, and rest as the boundaryless openness that's always already free of all content and identity.

The History of the Dream Metaphor

The metaphor of waking up from the darkness into the daylight, from the dream to reality—based as it is on our daily experience of shifting realities from sleep to waking—has a long history no doubt as old as humanity itself. In his famous allegory of the cave from the fifth century BCE, the Greek philosopher Plato describes a group of people chained since childhood to the interior of a cave and led to believe that the shadows cast on the cave wall constitute reality. If released from the cave and told that the sights they now saw, rather than the shadows, were real, he suggests, they would be confused at first and rush back to the cave and the comfortable illusion to which they'd become accustomed. But after prolonged exposure to the light of the sun they would finally recognize that they'd been inhabiting an illusory world and start to live from a new and radically different perspective.

In the East the dream metaphor can be traced back more than twenty-five hundred years to the Upanishads of Hinduism, the core texts of the Vedanta tradition of which Advaita is a part, and to the story of the Buddha, who lived in India a few hundred years later. His name means awakened one and his teachings urged his followers to awaken from the dream of separation and realize our essential inseparability from life itself. According to the early teachings of the Buddha, the illusory world from which we awaken is called samsara, the endless cycle of birth, death, and rebirth that's the inescapable hallmark of human existence.

Samsara is marked by impermanence and insubstantiality and is inherently unsatisfactory; we suffer because we attach to the idea of a separate self, struggle against the way things are by attaching to what we like and resisting what we don't like, and try to impose our own agenda on life. By acting in self-serving and unskillful ways, we create karma that ties us to the endless cycle of reincarnation. The suffering of samsara does not cease until, after years of meditation practice, we can awaken out of it into an abiding, peaceful state known as nirvana, free of attachment and aversion and undisturbed by the vicissitudes of the manifest world. Once nirvana is realized, the cycle of samsara driven by karma comes to an end, and we never reincarnate in any form, which is the mark of a truly awakened being, or *arhat*.

In Mahayana Buddhism this representation of samsara shifted with the recognition that the wheel of life, death, and rebirth is not inherently unsatisfactory—in fact it's both empty of substantiality yet inherently complete and perfect just as it is. Samsara is not separate from nirvana, and we can be awake in the midst of ordinary life, with all its complications, and experience the constant change without attachment or suffering. From this perspective, samsara is not the way the world itself works, it's the prison that the mind creates by weaving the narrative of a separate self that exists across time and holds us in its thrall. Freedom from samsara doesn't require stepping off the wheel of life, it just involves stepping out of the claustrophobic narrative created by the mind.

In the Hindu tradition of Advaita (or nondual) Vedanta, the notion of *maya* (literally, "illusion") cuts deeper still and teaches that the manifest world is not only misconstrued by the mind and interpreted through a thick narrative of beliefs, memories, and constructs—it's inherently illusory. This view is expressed in the well-known Advaita formulation that the world is an illusion, Brahman (the absolute) alone is real—and the world is nothing but Brahman. Only the pure, absolute, unmanifest reality exists, and the relative world of everyday life is just an illusory overlay on the absolute reality, like an imaginary snake superimposed by the viewer on a coiled piece of rope that causes fear until its true nature is revealed. Though both Advaita Vedanta and Mahayana Buddhism subscribe to the view (known as the two truths) that both absolute and relative reality exist and interpenetrate, Advaita seems to give greater weight to the absolute as the deeper and more fundamental reality.

Western Psychology and the Ego Tunnel

Over the past hundred years or so, the meeting of nondual teachings from the monasteries and ashrams of Asia with a postmodern sensibility informed by the scientific method and the insights of Western psychology has yielded some illuminating hybrid perspectives. For example, the Swiss psychiatrist C. G. Jung—whose ideas about self were influenced by his contact with Indian philosophy—believed we filter our experience of reality and other people through a thick veil of projections drawn from unconscious shadow parts of our psyche. According to Jung the process of maturation and individuation involves re-owning these projections and seeing reality more clearly, free of projection. In spiritual and New Age circles, the process of recognizing and acknowledging the shadow has gained popularity in recent years, particularly as a way to avoid bypassing our unresolved psychological issues and getting stuck in the transcendent.

Eastern teachings have likewise had an influence on existential, humanistic, transpersonal, and even cognitive psychologies. One of my teachers when I was a psychotherapist in training, the existential psychologist James Bugental, called the dream we inhabit the "self-and-world construct system" (SWCS), a complex edifice created by the mind to find meaning in an otherwise uncertain and incomprehensible world.[1] As a clinician he believed that a negative, distorted SWCS was the primary cause of his clients' suffering, and that the most effective way to free them from its grip was to challenge it again and again and help them to replace it with a more accurate and empowering construct.

In the direct approach to spiritual awakening, we're interested not in replacing the SWCS—a more accurate dream is still no more than a dream—but rather in recognizing it as just a mental representation and replacing it with direct, clear seeing into the nondual nature of reality. Still, the term "self-and-world construct system" is a potent, succinct, and nonjudgmental way of describing the dream we inhabit, whether we're seeking to eliminate it or to disidentify from it.

In the cognitive-behavioral approach so popular in therapeutic circles, especially for the treatment of depression, the problem lies in our schemas, our distorted core beliefs about self, world, and other people that make up our narrative and must be challenged and changed to align more closely with the way things are. Again, the emphasis is on changing them and keeping the self in place at the center of the psyche, but cognitive-behavioral therapy (CBT) can be helpful in guiding people halfway toward awakening by beginning the process of recognizing the persistent schemas that make up the dream.

Another helpful model, based on cutting-edge neuroscientific research, is the ego tunnel, a term coined by the German philosopher of consciousness Thomas Metzinger to refer to the cave (or dream) and the separate self that inhabits it. Drawing on a series of groundbreaking experiments in neuroscience, virtual reality, and robotics, Metzinger argues that the brain develops a phenomenal-self model (PSM) that is grounded in bodily feelings and necessary for controlling movement in the world. This model, he suggests, gives us the conscious experience of being someone, a first-person perspective. It's a "highly flexible entity" with global properties, and whatever is embedded in it is perceived as belonging to a me.[2] In other words, everything that appears to exist in the ego tunnel is taken to be an inextricable part of the particular dream I take to be myself. The phenomenal-self model includes a complex set of constructs through which we perceive reality but that can't be distinguished from reality itself. We live in a dream of our own devising with an illusory self at the center, but have the illusion that we're directly in contact with the real world.

According to Metzinger, conscious experience is an invisible interface, a transparent medium, and we're glued to the contents of our self model as if to a virtual-reality screen, just as the inhabitants of Plato's cave were riveted to the cave wall and did not realize there was anything beyond it. The ego tunnel appears to differ from the dream as articulated in the nondual wisdom teachings, however, because it's not something we can wake up from, aside from being aware of its limitations and the illusory nature of the separate self it conjures. It's hardwired into our nervous system and endemic to the human condition, and thus both empowers and limits us.

Pointer: The Problem with Emptiness

In my experience, many people have a hard time with the teaching of emptiness because it has nihilistic overtones and can be misunderstood to suggest meaninglessness or absence of value. In fact, emptiness is an elaboration of the essential recognition of impermanence—that is, reality can't be located or grasped, it has no inherent or enduring substantiality and eludes our attempts to pin it down or characterize it as it really is.

Some teachers use terms like openness, groundlessness, or even beingness to avoid the negative connotations of emptiness. In the Mahayana Buddhist tradition, including especially Zen, emptiness, *sunyata*, is often paired with and complemented by the term "suchness," *tathata*—that is, the indescribable and inherent fullness or perfection of what presents itself in each moment. Keep in mind that these complex and esoteric terms are merely pointers to a direct apperception that dawns beyond the mind. Don't get caught up in trying to figure emptiness out, just let the pointers act on you and discover for yourself what they evoke.

How the Dream Causes Suffering

As the Buddha taught, suffering in one form or another is endemic to the human condition; we inevitably get sick, age, and die, and along the way experience painful circumstances and heartbreaking losses. This is what Buddha called the "first arrow of suffering," which is unavoidable in a world of impermanence and constant change. No one is exempt, even the noble prince he once was before he renounced the pleasures of the palace and took up the life of a wandering seeker.

But the second arrow—sometimes called suffering as opposed to simple pain—derives from the stories we tell ourselves about life, the resistance to what is and the entrenched beliefs that it should be otherwise and could have been different, along with all the judgments, interpretations, ideas, misgivings, regrets, and expectations we pick up along the way. The second arrow arises only in the dream of separation woven by the mind. Reality itself can be painful, but suffering belongs only to the dream character still stuck in the illusion of duality, of inside and outside, self and other. As long as we believe we're separate from the rest of life, believe we're the fragment rather than the whole, we're going to suffer.

At the same time, there's the suffering and dissatisfaction inherent in living in the dream while knowing at some deep and intuitive level that it's an illusion, but not knowing how to break free. Many of the people who come to me for spiritual counseling report that they've felt since childhood that they didn't belong in this world, that they knew the consensus reality they shared with others was somehow a lie or a pretense, and that there was a deeper dimension of joy, love, and peace beneath all the dissatisfaction they witnessed around them. Walking in nature, listening to beautiful music, communing with a loved one, they intimated this deeper dimension beneath all appearance and yearned to return to their true home but didn't know how.

Then of course there's the incessant fear, anger, stress, resistance, and conflict that inevitably arise when we experience life in dualistic terms. If we believe we're a separate self in here with a seemingly separate world outside us, we end up mired in a constant struggle to get enough of what we think we need—love, approval, status, material possessions—and avoid what we believe to be threatening. Even the subtlest identification with a separate self can constellate a need to defend and protect our vulnerable position in opposition to others and the world outside. Beneath all the longing, ironically, what we really want—love, safety, happiness—is only available to us when we let go of expecting to get it from outside ourselves and turn within, to the source of all fulfillment, the recognition that we've never been separate even for an instant. In words attributed to the Buddha, happiness is wanting what you have and not wanting what you don't have.

This world we've woven in and around us is inherently dualistic, setting me against them, self against other, inside versus outside, desirable versus undesirable, and creating a split or division that's not easily bridged once it's mistaken for reality. Awakening, of course, bridges the divide and unites the opposites. But waking up once, no matter how decisively, is almost never enough to extinguish the dream for good. Once we've awakened out of this dream and seen it for what it is, we need to keep acknowledging our projections, memories, beliefs, and expectations but not believe or indulge them, and to endlessly return and refresh our connection with reality lest we fall asleep and forget once again.

Awakening from the Dream Again and Again

In the moment of awakening to our true nature beyond the separate self, we recognize that the dream we've constructed and inhabited our entire lives is just a fraction of the whole, an illusory construct with a me at the center that filters and obscures our inseparability from all of life. Once glimpsed, this profound insight into the nondual nature of reality can't be fully unseen, but it can and generally does retreat to the background as the dream reasserts itself and the demands of everyday life thrust us back into our accustomed roles and limited views. Developed and refined over a lifetime, the dream is extraordinarily tenacious at holding us in its thrall, and awakening is just the beginning of a lifelong process of seeing through the construct, falling under its spell again, then loosening its hold again, as we live more and more of the time in clarity and openness.

The narrative construct with a me at the center is as much a complex conceptual representation of what the world is like as it is a self-representation—indeed, they are intertwined and inseparable. Often affecting us in the subtlest of ways and functioning beneath the level of conscious awareness, it informs our every interaction and acts as a filter for our ongoing experience of life. As Western developmental psychology has persuasively demonstrated, this self-and-world construct has been deeply imprinted over a lifetime of conditioning, beginning in earliest childhood, and tends to get reinforced again and again as it shapes and reshapes our life as adults.

The process of deconstructing the dream has its own natural unfolding and momentum that can't be hurried or willed to completion. But it may certainly grind to a halt or even regress back to earlier stages of unconsciousness if we're not wholehearted in our dedication to seeing through the illusions and revealing the truth, no matter how uncomfortable it may be for the ego. Often suffering proves to be the most compelling motivator, because once we know the ease of being that arises when we live free of the dream, even the slightest reidentification may cause enough discomfort, angst, or dissatisfaction to drive us back to the deconstruction process again.

In practice, deconstructing the self is not necessarily an active, assertive dismantling requiring deep uncovering and investigation, though these may play a role. Rather, it's more a matter of seeing the dream for what it is— a complex narrative made up of thoughts, memories, images, and emotions—from the perspective of awareness itself, which is uninvolved in the process. The key is not to struggle to eliminate it, but simply to refuse to identify with it again and again. On an everyday level, this can take the form of what I call the four Rs: *Remember* to stop and reflect, *recognize* your natural state, *return* to wakefulness, and *rest* there. But first you would do well to become familiar with the dream you inhabit. (For more on welcoming experience just as it is, see chapter 7, page 149.)

Of course, some tentative self-and-world construct, some approximation of who we are and how the world works, is necessary at the relative level to enable us to function in our everyday lives. To be able to meet our fundamental wants and needs as a human being, we need to have a clear sense of what they are and a clear map of the territory we need to negotiate to meet them. But this construct can be flexible, open, informed by the awakened understanding of no self and interbeing, and subject to constant reality-testing and readjustment, rather than rigid, deeply rooted in the past, and based on a dualistic, self-centered view. Above all, we can adopt the construct not as an abiding identity but as a momentary formulation that we can let go of when it no longer applies. (For more on how to function in relationship from an awakened perspective, see chapter 9.)

Meditation: Remember, Recognize, Return, and Rest

The practice of effortless mindfulness—what I call resting and allowing—is an opportunity to step back from your ongoing argument with reality and let everything be just as it is. If you only engage in the practice for a short period each day, however, it won't have much of an effect on your ability to stay present in a consistent way. For this I recommend frequent, short reflections on what I call the four Rs:

- Stop from time to time and *remember* to notice the location and quality of your awareness right now. Is it tense or relaxed, fixated or open? Are you lost in the dream or present for what is?

- *Recognize* the awake awareness that's always already present beyond any deliberate effort to be aware.
- Let go of any fixation and *return* and *rest as awareness* in your natural state of inherent wakefulness.

Making this an ongoing practice cuts through the dream on a moment-to-moment basis and enables clear seeing free of projection and conceptual overlays.

Big Self, Small Self, No Self, and the Multiplicity of Selves

The term "self" is bandied about in both Western psychology and nondual spiritual traditions, and a thorough investigation of the similarities and differences in usage would require a volume unto itself and still not penetrate to the essence. The truth is, the English word "self" has been used to translate words from multiple languages—Sanskrit, Tibetan, Japanese, Latin, German—and the attempt to use it to mean very different realities across cultures, worldviews, and traditions has only generated more confusion. In this brief section I attempt to find some order in the chaos and refer us back again and again to the direct experience to which the term points.

Self/No Self from a Nondual Perspective

As we're exploring in this chapter, the dream we take to be reality centers on an illusory separate self around whom the dream is constructed. This is the self-and-world construct system described by the psychologist James Bugental, the ego tunnel of Thomas Metzinger, and the edifice that dissolved at the Buddha's enlightenment. In the Vedanta tradition, the sage realizes that this seemingly separate self, known as atman, is not other than the absolute reality, Brahman. *Tat tvam asi,* in the words of the Upanishads. That is what you are. The Buddha, who Hindus still consider a great Hindu sage, taught that in fact the self (atman) doesn't exist at all (anatman). It's an illusory construct superimposed on a reality marked by constant change, insubstantiality, and impermanence. No matter how closely and intensively we search, we cannot locate a separate self inside, nor can we find any lasting solidity or selfhood in the phenomenal world. Instead, we find the constantly changing contents of experience—thoughts, feeling, sensations, what the Buddha called the "five skandhas," or aggregates, of form, feelings, perceptions, volitions, and awareness—but nothing permanent or abiding.

Subsequent awakened masters in both traditions have tweaked and played with these terms. For Ramana Maharshi, the great Advaita sage of twentieth-century India, only atman, Self (with a capital S), exists; there is no (small s) self or other, no inside or outside, no separate ego or mind, only this one nondual reality in all its unicity, aware of itself. Self is what each of us is fundamentally, our essential spiritual nature beyond all duality. The direct experiential recognition of this truth—that "I am That," as the Upanishads put it—constitutes self-realization.

In the Buddhist Mahayana tradition, two separate currents emerged. One taught that everything, including the five skandhas that constitute both internal and external reality, is not only impermanent but empty and devoid of any inherent substantiality. Another promoted the insight that beneath all the constant change and insubstantiality lies an abiding essence or consciousness. These currents merged in the nondual traditions of Zen and Tibetan Dzogchen-Mahamudra. In Zen this essence, which is at the same time inherently empty, is known as true Self, big mind, or buddha nature, and we can realize it for ourselves in the experience of awakening, or kensho. In Tibetan Dzogchen it's called *rigpa*, the fundamental nature of mind, which is essentially empty, aware, and compassionate, and which the teacher points out directly to the disciple in intimate dialogue.

Ramana Maharshi and the great Zen and Dzogchen masters appear to be using very different terms to point to the same nondual reality. Whether we call it Self or emptiness, big mind or buddha nature, true Self or suchness, there is only the one without a second, dynamic and ever changing in manifestation and at the same time unchanging and undisturbed in essence. These are profound concepts, but they only have the power to transform our understanding of life if we make them our own through direct experience. This is the recognition that dawns in the moment of genuine awakening: that is, as I explained in chapter 1, there is no separate subject localized in here that's perceiving a reality out there, but only this one nondual reality—boundless, luminous, undivided, and all-pervasive—which is empty of substantiality and inherently awake to itself.

The Self to which the sages and masters point is an existential reality far beyond the usual confines of what constitutes a self in the psychological sense. Unlike the Western psychological self, which is a shadowy and elusive construct alleged but never really located or pinned down, Self can be directly experienced or intuited in a moment out of time, and the experience dismantles, or at least leaves in tatters, the dream we've constructed and substantially frees us from the fetters of self-clinging and self-identification.

Western Perspectives on Self

By contrast with the Eastern view, most discussions of self in Western psychology take for granted that we all have an intuitive sense of what the term "self" refers to and would agree that we could not function without one. For example, the entry "Self and Identity" from the *Oxford Research Encyclopedia of Psychology* describes self in this way:[3]

> The concept of the self has beguiled—and frustrated—psychologists and philosophers alike for generations. One of the greatest challenges has been coming to terms with the nature of the self. Every individual has a self, yet no two selves are the same. Some aspects of the self create a sense of commonality with others whereas other aspects of the self set it apart.

> The self usually provides a sense of consistency, a sense that there is some connection between who a person was yesterday and who they are today. And yet, the self is continually changing both as an individual ages and he or she traverses different social situations. A further conundrum is that the self acts as both subject and object; it does the knowing about itself. With so many complexities, coupled with the fact that people can neither see nor touch the self, the construct may take on an air of mysticism akin to the concept of the soul.

Nevertheless, the authors attempt to define the self as "a multifaceted, dynamic, and temporally continuous set of mental self-representations. These representations are multifaceted in the sense that different situations may evoke different aspects of the self at different times. They are dynamic in that they are subject to change in the form of elaborations, corrections, and reevaluations."

Rather than taking the self's existence for granted, as the authors of this definition do when they offhandedly say "everyone has a self," yogis and sages over the millennia have been led by its elusive, multifaceted, and insubstantial nature to subject this construct to profound and exhaustive investigation. After all, how can a single supposed entity, without substance or consistency, subject to constant change and completely different from person to person and moment to moment, actually be shown to exist? Understandably enough, their unanimous conclusion is that it can't and doesn't, it's just a convenient concept used to incorporate a host of functions and actions that don't have a separate someone at their core. Doing happens, as the teaching goes, but there is no doer thereof; thinking happens without a thinker; life happens through us but there's no one orchestrating the unfolding.

The direct experiential knowing that there's nothing but Self but no single self in charge gives rise to a freedom from grasping and identification, an openness without definition or restriction, a lightness of being, and an unshakable happiness and alignment with the way things are in the knowing that they could not be otherwise. When awareness is turned back upon itself, it cannot find a separate someone on the throne of consciousness, just an endlessly changing procession of viewpoints and perspectives, a multiplicity of selves rather than a singularity of self.

The entry "Self and Identity" goes on to formulate the distinction—first made by one of the founders of modern psychology, William James—between the I and the me, with the I being "self as agent, thinker, and knower, the executive function that experiences and reacts to the world, constructing mental representations and memories as it does so," and the me being "the individual one recognizes as the self, which for James included a material, social, and spiritual self"—that is, "the body, mind, and possessions, the various selves one may express and others may recognize depending on the social setting, and one's values, personality, beliefs about the self." Quite a complex of qualities and functions to fit neatly into a single term. Could it be in fact that there are multiple selves, as James suggests, contributing to our psychological complexity rather than a single self that contains it all?

Jungian Notion of "Self"

Before we answer that question, let's take a brief detour and discuss Jung's notion of self, which was influenced by his interest in Indian spirituality as well as his forays into astrology, the I Ching, and the archetypes of Western mythology. Originally a disciple of Freud, Jung broke with his teacher over the notion of "self," which in Freudian psychology is understood merely as another structure within the mind rather than as an independent entity in its own right. For Jung, the self is more than just a psychic structure, it's a dynamic force that brings the energy and intentions of the divine or transcendent to bear on the individual psyche and guides the individual on their journey through life. In this way it resembles the Self described by Ramana Maharshi.

In the Jungian view, the self goes far deeper than the conventional psychological understanding of self-image or executive function or sense of identity that gives consistency amid constant change. Rather, it brings what Jung called the "collective unconscious," the repository of conflicting transpersonal archetypes and energies, into direct contact with the individual psyche and helps integrate them into a coherent and functioning whole. It's a teleological force—that is, one that has its own sense of direction apart from what the individual might want, and the process of integration from a Jungian perspective, known as individuation, can be just as disturbing and disorienting to the individual as the process of spiritual awakening. When the self takes charge, the ego, which is seen as a mere reflection of the self, must step aside and ultimately surrender to a power greater than its own.

When I work with students individually or in groups, one question I'm often asked is: If there's no self, just being or consciousness without a separate someone in charge, how do I know how to act? What inner guidance system do I follow? I generally advise that they set aside the mind's ideas about what should happen next and consult a deeper voice or intuitive inner knowing that's centered in the heart or belly. But what deeper wisdom guides this knowing? The Buddhist tradition offers the notion of *prajna*, the "heart wisdom" that cuts through dualistic understandings and strikes to the essence of reality. But prajna is not quite the personal-level knowing we're talking about here. Jung's notion of self offers an answer from a Western psychological perspective.

According to Jung, the self is a force unique to each individual that runs deeper than ego and carries with it the power of archetypal forces and energies but isn't as universal as the Self of Ramana Maharshi or the true nature of Zen. When we follow the guidance of self at this level, the actions we take feel right and true and in alignment with who we are as an individual, but they're neither the universal truths of Self with a capital S nor the limited, fragmentary, and self-serving dictates of ego. They emerge from our sense of wholeness and interconnectedness rather than from the ego's self-centered perspective, yet my self is different from your self and guides my actions in particular ways. This level of knowing, somewhere between ego and the absolute, is often called "soul" in the Jungian tradition, not in the sense of a separate entity that transmigrates between lifetimes, but as a deeper heart wisdom and sense of destiny and purpose that's unique to each person.

The Multiplicity of Selves

If we examine our experience from moment to moment, we may notice that the thoughts, emotions, perspectives, and points of view are constantly coming and going in the dream. For example, one moment we may feel anxious and preoccupied about the future, the next moment we're completely relaxed because we believe all is well and trust that things will work out as planned. In the process, our self-image, our sense of self, may radically morph from being young and helpless to being wise and capable. And the stories we tell ourselves may not only differ but contradict and even mutually exclude one another. Beneath the illusion of being a solid separate me lies constant change.

Of course, we could interpret these changing states as merely the changing experiences of the separate self, different thoughts coming and going in and to an abiding and consistent me, as the author of the Oxford encyclopedia entry does. This is often the moment-to-moment experience in mindfulness meditation, for example. But if we look more closely, we may discover that the experiences are radically different from one another, as if they constituted not only different thoughts but completely different perspectives, different worldviews, different dreams. One explanation posed by Western psychology is that, instead of being a single, solid, separate self enthroned like a monarch in the center of the dream, we're constantly shifting our identity from one self to another as they move across the proscenium of consciousness, like the actors that Shakespeare described that "strut and fret their hour upon the stage, and then are heard no more"[4]—or at least not until the next time they have something to say.

This notion of rotating and interacting selves—called ego states, subpersonalities, or parts—has been developed and articulated over the decades by a number of different schools of psychology, first by

Jung in his notion of autonomous "feeling toned complexes," and most recently by an approach known as internal family systems. Buddha himself noted that, instead of a separate self, there are a multitude of states—called skandhas, or aggregates—that make up the illusion of a self. In the midst of this constant change, what does abide and afford continuity is the stage itself, the global awareness in which these parts or states come and go, which remains undisturbed and is always available to make experience possible. Once this greater awareness is recognized in a moment of awakening and realized to be our true nature, who we are fundamentally, our relationship to our inner experience transforms into one of welcoming rather than identification. There is no self, just a multitude of selves, each with its separate fragment or facet of the dream we take to be our life. In practice, this global awareness welcomes the selves and mediates the communication between them. (For more about these selves or parts and how to work with them, see chapter 7, page 149.)

Coming Home to Who You Really Are

Just as Plato likened the dream to a dark cave filled with shadows, the Buddha compared it to an edifice that keeps getting reconstructed lifetime after lifetime until the forces that lead to the endless construction project get seen through and eliminated. In his view, these forces are the so-called obscurations: indulgence in sensual pleasure, attachment to endless becoming, and ignorance of the true nature of reality. Later Buddhist formulations identify the obscurations as the three root mental states, or poisons, that cloud the mind and disturb the heart: attachment to what we want (leading to lust, jealousy, craving, and addiction); aversion to what we don't want (leading to anger, fear, and anxiety); and ignorance (leading to apathy, nihilism, and depression). When these forces are seen through and released, the endless building and rebuilding of the edifice of self and other, the dream realm of separation and isolation, comes to an end.

According to the scripture known as the Dhammapada, at the moment of his enlightenment the Buddha purportedly said, "Through many births I roamed without reward or rest, seeking the house-builder. Painful is birth again and again. House-builder, you've been seen! You will not build this house again. All your rafters are broken, the ridge pole has collapsed. The mind has reached the unconditioned, and craving has ceased."[5] From the perspective of traditional Buddhism, this meant he would no longer be bound to the wheel of samsara or endure any further reincarnations.

In the view of the direct approach as espoused by the nondual wisdom traditions, "craving" is not the primary problem and the "elimination" of defilements and obscurations is not required. Instead, we aim to see through the endless process of constructing and reconstructing without identifying with the narrative being constructed, remaining awake and alert amidst all the arising as the dream loses its hold over our lives and the clarity of deep insight into the nondual nature of reality dawns amidst the dark. Primordial awareness, our essential nature, is the powerful force or light that frees us from the stranglehold of samsara.

Awakening to our essential nature (described in detail in chapters 1, page 9, and 2, page 27) is the fruition of the journey and the key that frees us from the dream. Instead of struggling to purify ourselves and achieve a kind of perfect state of mind, as traditional Theravada Buddhism enjoins, we're turning the light of awareness back upon itself to realize the essential light and love that lies at the core of our being and has never been absent even for a heartbeat.

In the world's spiritual traditions this circular odyssey of setting out only to turn back to where we began is likened to the journey of the prodigal son or daughter, the young man or woman who sets forth into the world to find their fortune only to discover, after long and arduous seeking, that they had a fortune buried under their own hearth all along, or a diamond sewn into their pocket by a benevolent father that they hadn't noticed before. Somehow, though, the seeking appears to be a required stage in the journey that makes returning and recognizing possible. As an old adage puts it, the truth can't be found through seeking, but only seekers end up finding it.

Often we're drawn naturally and spontaneously to this journey by a yearning that begins quite young to reconnect with the source from which we came, our true home that we've lost touch with and seek to rediscover. "Our birth is but a sleep and a forgetting" of the "celestial light" of our true spiritual nature, writes Wordsworth in famous lines from his poem "Ode: Intimations on Immortality."[6] In my own case, I had a recurring childhood dream of wandering around the neighborhood where we lived, knocking on every door, hoping to find my true home but never being welcomed in. "From my home in the hills, why do I roam," laments the singer Jai Uttal, "to my home in the hills, take me back."[7]

What About Ego?

The terms "ego" and "self" have sometimes been used interchangeably in spiritual circles, but I would like to suggest a fundamental distinction between them, based on both Buddhist wisdom and Western psychological thought. As we've discussed, the separate self is a construct that takes center stage in the dream we inhabit but can't be located through introspection and has no substantial identity in and of itself. By contrast, ego, as described by Freud and other psychologists, is not an entity but a function or activity that mediates between our needs and desires and the external world, while moderating and responding to the strictures of the inner critic, the superego. The ego makes it possible for us to negotiate the world successfully, to take care of ourselves and our family, to make choices based on what may benefit or disadvantage us, and to fulfill our intentions, both spiritual and secular. Without a healthy ego, we wouldn't be able to listen to teachings, practice meditation or self-inquiry, choose a teacher, or wake up to our essential spiritual nature.

Here's what the Western Theravada Buddhist monk Thanissaro Bhikku has to say about ego: "The test of how far your wisdom has matured lies in the strategic skill with which you can keep yourself from doing things that you like to do but that would cause long-term harm, and the skill with which you can talk yourself into doing things that you don't like to do but that would lead to long-term well-being and happiness. In other words, mature wisdom requires a mature ego."[8]

At the same time, paradoxically, ego is the manager of the self-and-world construct system and perpetuates the narrative by giving credit for everything that happens in our lives to the illusory self at the center. Just as a male cat sprays the trees in its territory to claim them as its own, or a two-year-old says "me" and "mine" about everything in their purview, ego marks each experience with the imprint of self. It's a servant of the dream but not the master, devoted to keeping it running and completely enthralled by what it serves.

Since it thoroughly believes in the existence of the separate self and devotes its energies to maximizing its benefits and minimizing its losses, the ego will go to whatever lengths necessary to make sure the (illusion of) self survives and thrives—unless, that is, it's tempered and schooled by a greater wisdom and a devotion to a greater good beyond the separate self. This wish for the benefit of all may arise from a deeper ground than ego, but ego in the sense of a healthy reality function and sense of agency is required to implement it.

Without this wisdom, the ego will quickly turn self-serving into self-absorption, or what Buddhists call "self-clinging." The ego is a necessary function, but it needs to be educated, ripened, and matured through spiritual awakening. In moderation, it takes good care of this body-mind and the others in its world. In excess, it benefits the body-mind to the exclusion of everything and everyone else and turns self-care into narcissism and self-indulgence.

In its attempts to take care of us and protect us from suffering, ego often causes as much suffering as it relieves by becoming attached to its own agenda and struggling against the way things are. The Tibetan teacher Chögyam Trungpa defined ego as struggle; I like to say it's the resistance to what is. It's also the seat of what Buddhists call the three poisons of attachment, aversion, and ignorance, and it thrashes about and puts up quite a fuss when things don't go its way, which they rarely do.

Despite what some spiritual teachers may suggest, however, ego is not the enemy, and pitting ourselves against it in an attempt to eliminate it and become egoless just creates an inner conflict between parts of the ego that can't be resolved. Rather, we can see it for what it is without trying to change it, while infusing it with the greater wisdom and love we discover as we awaken. When we realize our inseparability with all of life, ego devotes itself to aligning with rather than resisting what is and takes action based not on narrow self-interest but on the good of the larger Self we now know ourselves to be.

Of course, all of this needs to be taken with a grain of salt, as an ideal to be aspired to but not often realized in a consistent way. First, like the self, ego can't be located or grasped. It's an elusive and insubstantial force that's not easily reprogrammed from its appointed mission of maintaining the dream and protecting the self. Its role is to get what it wants no matter the price, and human life—and human history—is writ large with the battles of very large egos. Though we may not be able to eliminate it, the point of spiritual practice is to re-educate the ego and loosen its grip as we abide more and more fully in awakened awareness, at one with the flow and unfolding of life.

Reflect and Inquire

Spend some time reflecting on the dream narrative you inhabit. Who do you take yourself to be? How do you define yourself? What is your self-image? What stories do you repeatedly tell yourself and others—about life, about yourself, about other people? And how do these stories distort reality and limit how you think and behave? How do they cause you suffering by limiting your ability to connect with life as it is?

As you go about your day, be aware of how this narrative, this self-and-world construct, keeps recreating and reinforcing itself in your inner dialogue, the repetitive thoughts that run through your mind and purport to tell you what's true. These are the people I need to deal with, you say to yourself, the problems I need to solve, the positions I need to protect and defend. Notice how this construct causes you to react and interact with others.

Are these habitual thoughts true? Are they an accurate representation of reality? Do they constitute your true identity, who you really are? Or are they just the mind chatter that's so convincing and distracts you from recognizing the truth of who you are? And who are you really?

Q&A

Q: You talk about reality versus the dream, but isn't each person's reality always based on their dream? Is there such a thing as a reality untouched by the dream?

A: Reality exists in its own mysterious, unpredictable, and inimitable way, beyond our ability to fully comprehend it. Most of the time, we only perceive it through the filter of the beliefs, expectations, concepts, and conditioning we project upon it. Ultimately, when the illusion of separation falls away, seer and seen are realized to be two sides of the same coin, two expressions of the one nondual reality. In this reality, there's no separate someone seeing and nothing separate seen. There is just seeing, just perceiving, just the flow of life endlessly unfolding. We may never fully know reality—what my Zen teacher Suzuki Roshi called "things as it is"—but we can live a life of divine not-knowing. In words attributed to the Advaita sage H. W. L. Poonja, "I'm in love with the mystery, and I don't know what it is."

Can you or I ever see reality with utmost clarity and live from this nondual realization consistently, throughout our lives? Almost certainly not, but certainly we can have sustained glimpses and prolonged periods of no-separation that inspire, transform, and illuminate each moment. In any case, you can live in the deep recognition that reality is what you are—you are the wave at one with the limitless ocean of being of which you are merely an expression. As my teacher Jean Klein used to say, you can never know reality fully, but you can be it knowingly.

Q: Does the illusory self include the physical body? Are you saying that our physical bodies don't exist?

A: Even in the relative world of time and space, the separate self can't be located—it's just a construct, an imaginary locus of identity without even relative substantiality or solidity. By contrast, the body clearly exists on a relative level, otherwise awareness would not have a vehicle to express itself through, and of course you would not have a life as a person in the world.

But you might take a moment to examine the nature of the body you think you have. Most of what you imagine you know about the body is secondhand knowledge that you've been taught or read about online or in books. Here's my liver, here's how it functions, and here's what's wrong with it. I have high blood pressure and that means I need to eat less cholesterol, etc. Beyond these concepts and interpretations, all you can know about the body is through sensation—a heaviness here, a tightness there, a thickening here. Out of these direct sensations and acquired conceptual knowledge the mind cobbles together the construct called "my body." But all you can really know for certain is your experience right now, which is constantly changing.

Meditation: Investigating Your Thoughts

You may believe that you know what thoughts are, but do you really? Perhaps you've been told that they're the result of nerve impulses in the brain. But what is your direct experience? Sit quietly, settle comfortably, and spend a few minutes being aware of the coming and going of your breath. Now shift your awareness to your thoughts.

Thoughts are constantly arising and passing. In fact, we often complain that we're besieged by thoughts, but we rarely stop to explore them. They seem so real and solid, but when you turn toward them, we may find that they elude your grasp.

Begin by noticing whether your thoughts are largely visual or auditory. Do you tend to hear your thoughts, or see them, or a little of both? No doubt you find these questions strange. You may never have asked these questions of your thoughts before.

Do your thoughts have color, shape, size, density, volume? Where are your thoughts located? Do they seem to be happening inside your head, or outside your head, or somewhere else, or inside or outside your body? Can you find them? Can you locate them? Where do your thoughts come from? Can you locate their source?

And where do they go when they're no longer there? What happens to your thoughts when you try to examine them closely in this way? Do they stay still, or do they elude your investigation?

Notice that each thought refers to another thought, to a thought about the past or a thought about the future. Thoughts refer to thoughts refer to thoughts, thoughts about others, thoughts about ourselves. They're constantly referring to one another in this intricate network of interrelated self-referential thoughts. This network is the dream you inhabit, the narrative you weave, the story you tell about your life.

But where is the supposedly solid, separate someone inside to whom these thoughts and feelings refer? Can you locate it? Is there a there there? Or is this apparent separate someone just a collection of more thoughts and feelings constantly shifting and changing?

Everything you take yourself to be—your ideas, your beliefs, your past history, future plans, aspirations, stories, feelings, preferences, etc.—are merely thoughts arising and passing away, ungraspable, nonlocatable.

Now ask yourself, who or what is aware of these thoughts and feelings? You can talk about your beliefs, your feelings, your memories, your ideas, because they're objects of your experience. But can you find the one who is aware of them, the ultimate subject? Can this subject ever become an object of your experience? What do you discover? Notice what you're left with when you can't find the one who is aware. How does this affect you?

Rest in this not finding, this not knowing, for a few moments or more, then go about your day.

7

Welcoming What Is

During my years as a Zen Buddhist monk, one of my teachers urged us to develop what he called "the power of samadhi," a concentrated, samurai-like mind-state that would enable us to cut through delusion and penetrate the meaning of the Zen stories, or koans, that purportedly conceal the mysteries of life. As instructed, I learned to become one-pointed and managed to solve a few hundred of the more than seven hundred koans on the syllabus, but over time my meditation became tight, narrow, and lacking in aliveness and joy. After a few years of this way of practicing I realized I couldn't continue without burning out and left to study Western psychology—and seek other approaches to awakening.

After dabbling in vipassana meditation and other methodologies far afield from meditation, I happened upon a teacher of Advaita Vedanta who counseled me to give up my habitual meditation technique and my tendency to exert effort and concentrate. Instead, he counseled, "open to the openness" that's already taking place and welcome whatever arises. Trained as a classical violinist and musicologist, the teacher, Jean Klein, likened this approach to meditation to the ambient, omnidirectional awareness involved in listening. When we listen in a relaxed way, he noted, we can't easily locate or pin down the sounds, they happen all around us, and the only way to include and appreciate them is to open our senses wide and allow them to come to us rather than concentrating on them or going out to get them.

Shortly after starting to meditate in this way, I had the powerful and life-changing realization that I am this openness itself rather than the separate someone being open or the content the openness contains. At last, here was the awakening or kensho I had strived so strenuously to achieve through concentration in all my years of Zen practice, presenting itself to me without effort. In the Soto Zen tradition, where I began, the core practice is known as *shikantaza*: just sitting. No effort, no achieving, no meditator, nothing meditated on, just being fully present at every level and letting everything be as it is. But I had never really understood how to do it because I was accustomed to making so much effort. Jean had revealed the essence of shikantaza, a kind of nonmeditation where simply being present merges with Being itself.

Jean called this quality of wholehearted, whole-body presence "welcoming." Whereas deliberate mindfulness involves focusing awareness on a particular object, welcoming is more receptive, global, and all inclusive. The emphasis is not on the object but on the welcoming itself, which is both a function and activity that one can do and at the same time a quality of being. Welcoming begins with simply allowing what is, as shikantaza instructs, and adds a heart-centered dimension of curiosity and warmth that lends intimacy to the process of being present. The Indian sage Nisargadatta Maharaj was referring to welcoming when he reportedly said, "Affectionate awareness is the crucial factor that brings reality into focus."

But welcoming is not only a particular way of being with our experience, it's also intrinsic to awareness itself. By its very nature, awareness welcomes what is, just as the sky welcomes whatever arises within it, and we merely need to align ourselves with our intrinsic wakefulness and join it. The ego, by its nature, is resistant to what is. If, on the other hand, you rest back and allow everything to be as it is with openness and curiosity but without effort, as Nisargadatta suggests, the deeper nature of reality will reveal itself to you. In the words of the Third Patriarch of Zen, Seng Ts'an, "The Great Way [of awakening] is not difficult for those not attached to preferences. When neither love nor hate arises, all is clear and undisguised. Separate by the smallest amount, however, and you are as far from it as heaven is from earth. If you wish to know the truth, then hold to no opinions for or against anything."[1]

By contrast, when we're trapped in the dream, we can't see the truth because our minds and hearts are closed by multiple layers of beliefs, preconceptions, judgments, preferences, and opinions that filter and obscure the way things are. We're too busy interpreting, attaching, and resisting what is and struggling to impose our agenda on life to stop and be present. We don't have enough trust and ease of being to let go of the struggle, even for a moment, and welcome. From the perspective of the dream, anything beyond its boundaries is not a guest but a potential enemy or friend. Hence the attitude of welcoming cuts through the dream at its source.

Being Human Is a Guesthouse

Perhaps the best description of the quality of attention at the heart of welcoming comes not from a Zen text or an Advaita Vedanta sutra, but from a poem by the eleventh-century Sufi poet Rumi, in which he offers detailed guidance in how to welcome our experience, both inner and outer. Let's explore this poem together, in a translation by the American poet Coleman Barks, and find out what it has to teach us.

The Guest House[2]

This being human is a guest house.
Every morning a new arrival.

A joy, a depression, a meanness,
some momentary awareness comes
as an unexpected visitor.

Welcome and entertain them all!
Even if they're a crowd of sorrows,

who violently sweep your house
empty of its furniture,
still, treat each guest honorably.
He may be clearing you out
for some new delight.

The dark thought, the shame, the malice,
meet them at the door laughing,
and invite them in.

Be grateful for whoever comes,
because each has been sent
as a guide from beyond.

What does being the host of a guesthouse really entail? What does it mean to have a place where people you've never met before and may not like or understand come and go freely, and at times unexpectedly, under your supervision and care? By entertain, of course, he doesn't necessarily mean amuse or divert, though those activities may be included as well. Rather, he seems to be using the word in the sense of trying out a new and unfamiliar thought to see how it resonates, getting to know in a curious and noncommittal way without agreeing or disagreeing, attaching or rejecting.

Above all, it means treating each guest with respect, honoring the validity and autonomy of the many energies and voices that frequent your abode because you're open to the new perspectives they bring and willing to let them guide and change you. At the same time, you don't get caught up in the dark and tumultuous drama they may perpetuate but remain rooted in your own intrinsic happiness and peace of mind and heart. Instead of imposing your preferences and preconceptions, you let things be as they are in their own way. "Obey the nature of things (your own nature)," teaches Seng Ts'an, "and you will walk freely and undisturbed. When the fundamental nature of things is not recognized, the mind's essential peace is disturbed to no avail. . . . The Way is perfect, as vast space is perfect, where nothing is lacking and nothing is in excess. Indeed, it is due to our grasping and rejecting that we do not know the true nature of things. Be serene and at one with things, and erroneous views will disappear by themselves."[3]

Compressed into this brief poem, Rumi offers, directly or by implication, some powerful pointers for relating with our ongoing experience from an awakened perspective:

- Guidance for how to be with our inner experience in an awakened way that frees us from identification while respecting the autonomy of the energies and voices.
- Detailed instruction for working with difficult emotions and embracing and harmonizing the inner family of selves.
- Radical self-acceptance and embrace of our karmic bundle.
- Direct pointers to our natural state of nondual presence.

Let's unpack each of the poem's implications one by one.

Being with Experience in an Awakened Way

In the Chinese Zen (Chan) tradition, the metaphor of host and guest appears in a number of teachings and koans to refer to the relationship between the relative and absolute dimensions. This is precisely what Rumi has in mind. In this poem the content of our experience, our thoughts and feelings, beliefs and stories, memories and expectations, are being hosted by the limitless openness of awakened awareness, our true nature, like guests at an inn. We don't need to do anything to make this happen, it's always already the case. But we can awaken to it and join it, allowing our individual awareness to merge with the openness of the absolute, like wave merging with ocean. One of my Zen teachers, Shunryu Suzuki Roshi, used to describe the practice of welcoming like this: Leave your front door and your back door open. Allow your thoughts to come and go. Just don't serve them tea or get caught up in the stories they tell.

In another version of the metaphor, from the *Surangama Sutra* popular in the Zen tradition, one of the Buddha's chief disciples shares his wisdom: "World-Honored One, suppose a visitor stops at an inn for a night or for a meal. Once his stay is ended or the meal is finished, he packs his bags and goes on his way. He's not at leisure to remain. But if he were the innkeeper, he would not leave. By considering this example of the visitor, the one who comes and goes, and the innkeeper, the one who remains, I understood what the visitor signifies. He represents transience"[4]—and by implication the one who remains, the host, is the awake, aware presence that does not come and go.

As the host, consciousness/awareness is in love with and intimately embraces its expressions on the manifest level because they are inseparable, not two, just as form is no other than emptiness, and emptiness no other than form, in the words of the *Heart Sutra* of Mahayana Buddhism. From this perspective, reality is the *lila*, or divine play, of absolute and relative in intimate embrace, or of Shiva and Shakti in the archetypal symbolism of nondual tantra.

Pointer: All or Nothing?

The twentieth-century Indian sage Nisargadatta Maharaj taught that when you look within and see that you are nothing, there is wisdom. When you look without and see that you are everything, there is love. And between these two your life flows. By looking deeply into the nature of the self-and-world construct, you discover that there's no separate self on the seat of consciousness, only boundless awareness that welcomes all arising like a host welcoming its guests. This is the wisdom of self-realization. By turning attention outward and delving into the mystery of manifestation, you discover that this nonseparation characterizes your relationship with all phenomena—in the words of the *Heart*

Sutra, form is emptiness and emptiness is form. "Gazing with sheer awareness into sheer awareness," says the Tibetan teaching poem "Tilopa's Song to Naropa," "habitual abstract structures melt into the fruitful springtime of awakening."[5] In other words, the concepts that constellate separation fall away and your essential oneness reveals itself. You're both nothing and everything, empty of substance yet boundlessly full of manifest reality. This profound paradox must be realized directly to be understood.

Working with Difficult Emotions and Mind-States

As Rumi suggests, being human is, by its very nature, a guesthouse inevitably visited by an endless progression of experiences both positive and negative, pleasant and painful, difficult and easy, simple and complex. Though we may blame ourselves for the content of our experience and draw conclusions and judgments about the kind of person we are based on the experiences we have, in fact we have no control of who and what comes and goes. Thoughts and feelings, beliefs and stories, arise in their own mysterious and often inexplicable way and present themselves to our awareness. How can we possibly know what experience we should be having? We're having the experience we have, and it may be cleaning us out for some new delight.

The challenge on the path of awakening is to meet each experience without identification or attachment, without pushing it away or attaching ourselves to it, with the welcoming presence that loves and receives them all and then frees them to release and move on. Otherwise, our identification with them adds more layers to the thick walls of the dream bubble that keeps us captive and prevents us from directly experiencing reality as it is with awakened eyes and ears. And if we have difficulty welcoming, as we understandably may, we can welcome with love and compassion our reluctance or inability to welcome.

Powerful negative emotions fueled by a lifetime of conditioning, however, can easily overwhelm our fragile and emergent ability to welcome, even after years of meditation and awakening. When such emotions arise and persist, there are several techniques that have proven especially helpful for investigating them and releasing their hold. The first, known by its acronym RAIN and developed by the mindfulness teachers Michele McDonald and Tara Brach, outlines four steps to working with challenging emotions and mind-states: recognizing the experience, allowing it to be as it is, investigating it briefly, and nurturing ourselves with self-compassion. This approach constitutes a form of true welcoming because it enriches mere allowing with the heart qualities of love and compassion. Here are the four stages of the RAIN meditation:

- *Recognize* the thoughts, feelings, and behaviors that are affecting you now.
- *Allow* the experiences you recognize to be there without trying to fix or avoid anything. If you recognize fear, for example, you might add the step of allowing by pausing, taking a deep breath, and simply saying "yes" or "this too."
- Drawing on your natural desire to know the truth, *investigate* by directing more focused attention to your present experience. Deepen the investigation by asking: How do I experience this in the body? What most wants my attention now? If possible, drop the conceptualizing and let awareness rest on the felt sense in the body.
- Once you've acknowledged your suffering, *nurture* yourself by directing self-compassion and care to your inner life. For example, you might ask what the wounded, frightened, or hurt place inside you needs most, and then offer some gesture of active care that addresses this need—reassurance, forgiveness, companionship, love. Experiment and see which intentional gesture of kindness most helps to comfort, soften, or open your heart.

When you've completed the active steps of RAIN, notice the quality of your presence now and rest in that open, wakeful, tender space. The RAIN exercise can free you from any limiting sense of self and re-acquaint you with the mystery and natural freedom of your own being.[6]

My teacher Jean Klein used to recommend that we first set aside the story that invariably lurks in the background fueling the difficult emotion, usually an argument with reality, a belief that things shouldn't be as they are (or should be otherwise), or a projection or interpretation that isn't entirely accurate. "She shouldn't have hurt me the way she did, he doesn't love me, they're taking advantage of me," etc. Then, Jean would instruct, remove the label from the experience, because words like "fear" and "anger" carry their own emotional valence and implicit judgment or blame and prevent us from experiencing the energy of the experience directly. Finally, he would suggest, just be with the emotion fully as a bodily felt experience and allow it to unfold and dissipate in awareness without interference or interpretation. (For a fuller description of this approach, see the meditation "Welcoming Difficult Emotions" on page 168.) In the Tibetan Buddhist tradition this is known as self-liberation: Emotions naturally release if they're allowed to be as they are and not held in place by the labels, judgments, and stories fabricated by the mind.

The Tibetan practice known as *tonglen* ("taking and sending") teaches how to transform painful or difficult emotions, experiences, interactions, and circumstances—first for others, then for yourself—through the power of bodhichitta (awakened heart).[7] Instead of taking in the positive and breathing out the negative, as you're taught to do in some New Age meditations, you breathe in the pain and darkness and breathe out love and light and extend it to yourself and others. In the process, you expand the love in your heart and empower yourself to be more compassionate in future.

Harmonizing the Inner Family of Selves

As we become accustomed to welcoming our inner experience, we may find that certain clusters of thoughts and emotions don't just come and go but have more lasting consistency and duration, as if they were separate ways of experiencing reality, separate dreams, or separate subpersonalities or selves. Buddhist and yogic psychologies don't pay attention to such larger, more enduring psychological units or divisions because they're exclusively focused on liberation rather than personal development. For this reason, they tend to limit their interest to thoughts, feelings, sensations, and other subtler and more transitory experiences where liberation reveals itself.

In the West the Swiss psychiatrist C. G. Jung pioneered the understanding of separate subpersonalities with what he called "feeling-toned complexes," autonomous clusters of emotionally charged psychological content that often have a transpersonal, archetypal dimension and work at cross-purposes to the conscious mind. For Jung they included the hero, mother and father, brother and sister, and anima (archetypal feminine) and animus (archetypal masculine). Other, more humanistic or transpersonal schools of Western psychology, like Gestalt, transactional analysis, psychosynthesis, and ego state psychology, have elaborated on the similar insight that we are composed of different parts that we're not fully aware of but that have a powerful and unrecognized impact on our attitudes, actions, and relationships.

One popular contemporary incarnation of this approach, internal family systems (IFS), teaches that each of us is a collection (or family) of autonomous parts (or selves) that have different independent worldviews, agendas, and roles. These parts, including inner children and inner protectors, have often developed in response to being wounded or traumatized in some way by early life experiences, and they're frequently in conflict with one another. The way to heal the conflict, according to IFS, is to welcome the parts, encourage them to give voice to their feelings and experiences, and afford them the love and recognition they never had and so desperately crave.

For example, say you're asked to give an important presentation at work. One part of you may feel excited and energized by the opportunity to demonstrate your competence and expertise. But another, more primitive part that's rooted in childhood experiences of being humiliated by a parent may be terrified of being criticized or rejected, and another part may be drowning out the competent part with messages of self-judgment and shame. As a result, you freeze up with anxiety and can't focus on the task at hand. You may try to willfully suppress or ignore these conflicting parts and push ahead despite the anxiety, which generally only serves to intensify it and buries the ongoing conflict rather than resolving it.

Alternatively, you could take the time to listen to the different parts and invite them to express their feelings, the points of view and life experiences on which those feelings are based, and the important role the parts have played in your development. Once you've listened to them carefully and wholeheartedly, you could validate their experience as you would a friend's and give them your unconditional love and support. The part that's able to extend love and support to the others but does not need any itself is known in IFS as "the Self." The Self from an IFS perspective is not the center of the psyche but just another part, one that represents the deeper knowing of our nondual, nonseparate spiritual nature. By welcoming and loving the other parts just as they are, the Self part heals the fissures and divisions in the psyche and brings harmony and order to the internal family of parts.

The understanding that we have multiple small selves that are often in conflict and need to be reconciled and healed is not at all incompatible with the deeper knowing that there is no single, substantial, separate self in the center of consciousness. In this view, the ego that works to maximize our self-interest (see chapter 6) is just one or a number of separate members of the family of parts. The more we can return and rest in the open, receptive, and nonjudgmental awareness of the Self as described by IFS—effectively identical with the awakened awareness that welcomes our inner experience just as it is—the freer we are of the tyranny of any one part or separate self. This approach embraces both the absolute dimension of pure wakefulness and the relative dimension of our complexity and multiplicity.

According to the founder of IFS, Richard Schwartz, the welcoming awareness of the Self enables us to bring harmony to the system by unburdening the parts of the pain they've accumulated from the past. "Basically, what I found is that love is the answer in the inner world, just as it is in the outer world. Listening to, embracing, and loving parts allows them to heal and transform as much as it does for people. In Buddhist terms, IFS helps people become bodhisattvas of their psyches in the sense of helping each inner sentient being (part) become enlightened through compassion and love."[8]

Embracing Our Karmic Bundle

Many of us turn to the pathless path because we're tired of suffering and feel motivated to change our lives in fundamental ways. Frustrated with our own all-too-human limitations, we aspire to emulate the great masters of old or the teachers we watch or listen to online. Mix in the almost universal tendency toward ruthless self-criticism and we may end up on an endless wheel of perfectionism, struggling to be like the Buddha or Ramana Maharshi and comparing ourselves unfavorably to some spiritual ideal while rejecting our own genuine wisdom and compassion because we don't believe they measure up.

The practice of welcoming offers the perfect antidote to this common tendency toward self-rejection and spiritual perfectionism. Indeed, welcoming is more than just a practice, it's a fundamental attitude toward life. As I said earlier, awareness by its very nature is already welcoming what is, we just need to join the welcoming that's always already taking place. In welcoming, we're saying yes to what is without reservation, not trying to pick and choose but embracing what arises without resistance or argument. In the words of the Third Patriarch Seng Ts'an, "If you wish to know the truth, then hold to no opinions for or against anything. To set up what you like against what you dislike is the disease of the mind." And again: "The Way is perfect, as vast space is perfect, where nothing is lacking and nothing is in excess. Indeed, it is due to our grasping and rejecting that we do not know the true nature of things."[9]

Believe it or not, this innate perfection includes the imperfect human beings right here, with all our apparent faults, shortcomings, and mistakes. Rather than recommending a path of self-perfection, the journey of awakening teaches us to accept ourselves fully just as we are—including, paradoxically, our resistance to accepting ourselves. To be enlightened, says Seng Ts'an, is not to be perfect, but to "not worry about perfection or non-perfection."[10]

Pointer: Welcoming Appropriate Action and Change

Welcoming is not psychological acceptance or resignation and doesn't imply that you agree with the way things are. It's just a clear-eyed acknowledgment of the way life is moving, including the actions you may feel moved to take to change or improve life in the way you see fit. Once you welcome the situation wholeheartedly, you're free to act in a realistic and appropriate way.

In other words, saying yes to what *is* sometimes means saying yes to saying no, based on your intuitive knowing that certain situations, behaviors, or people don't serve you or others well and you need to set boundaries or back away from involvement. This clear inner knowing, called prajna (heart wisdom) in Zen, often bypasses the rational, analytical mind and illuminates the way forward directly.

Of course, the question of how to take appropriate action that's both in alignment with your deepest spiritual understanding and principles and yet adequate to the circumstances on the relative level is one of the oldest

> spiritual conundrums, addressed in the earliest religious texts like the Bhagavad Gita and the story of Abraham and Isaac in the Old Testament. The practice of welcoming doesn't imply passivity, resignation, or complacency, but it does involve the recognition that life unfolds in its own mysterious way, beyond your conscious control, and couldn't be otherwise than the way it is–not because it's perfect according to some preestablished standard, but because this is the way the universe intends it to be.
>
> Welcoming reality includes welcoming your resistance to the way it is and your intuitive sense that it should be otherwise, which may naturally lead you to take action according to your preferences and predilections. Most important, from an awakened perspective you're called upon to act in alignment with the good of the whole, not just out of your own self-interest, and without attachment to getting what you want, as the Bhagavad Gita makes clear.

In Rumi's poem, the one who welcomes is the host, but the guests, once acknowledged, may move us to act in a variety of ways. This is a paradox the mind can't figure out in advance, and you can only welcome wholeheartedly and see where it takes you. As the Advaita sage Ramana Maharshi teaches, immerse yourself in the living present and the future will take care of itself.

In my years as both a psychotherapist and a spiritual teacher, I've found that our fundamental character and personality—based on certain inherited tendencies, idiosyncrasies, and limitations and forged over a lifetime of early conditioning and ongoing life experience—is remarkably resistant to change. We may be able to tweak it, improve it, harmonize it, or relax it, but the fundamental elements tend to remain more or less the same. We didn't choose it and we're not to blame for it, it was handed to us when we left home as a kind of karmic bundle that may take the rest of our lives to unpack and come to terms with, the grist in our mill of spiritual transformation, our teacher on the path of relationship. Facing the intractable isness of the way we are humbles and softens us and relieves us of our illusion that we can impose our agenda on life. It affords us the opportunity to surrender to the deeper order of the mystery that's always been in charge.

In my own case, for example, I would say that I'm a completely different person from the anxious, diffident young man who began to meditate more than fifty years ago. At the same time, and often much to my chagrin, the same habits of mind and reactive emotions keep recurring. What has fundamentally changed is my relationship to them: They arise in the space of awakened awareness and are seen for what they are, but I don't attach to them or indulge in them—at least most of the time. Being an imperfect human being, not a fully realized Buddha, I do occasionally act them out in unskillful ways. Now, however, I acknowledge the misunderstanding and reactivity, open my heart to my own karmic bundle, apologize, and move on.

Embracing our karmic bundle in this way also allows us to welcome and value our unique gifts and strengths, the particular ways that consciousness or true nature expresses itself through this bodymind rather than another. At the relative level, each of us came into being as a wave differentiating itself from the ocean with a particular purpose or life direction that we may or may not recognize but that often takes shape early in life through our interests and predilections, the things we love doing, studying, or expressing. If we look back, we may recall the moment we felt drawn to pick up a musical instrument or a tennis racquet, collect butterflies or write poetry, tinker with an engine or play with a chemistry set—not because we were told to but for some mysterious reason that would influence or define the trajectory of our lives. Each of us is not only inherently empty of self, we are also at the same time one precious and irreplaceable facet of the multidimensional jewel of being, with our own unique talents and tendencies. And we are deserving of love just for being who we are.

Pointer: Welcoming Nondual Presence

In the end, welcoming is not just a practice or an attitude to add to our experience, both inner and outer, it's a description of the inherent nature of awake awareness itself. On a retreat many years ago I had the unexpected realization that consciousness delights in its expressions in form because it's not separate from them and sees itself reflected in them, as a mother or father sees themselves reflected in the eyes of their child. In the Western Abrahamic traditions, God expresses the same delight in Genesis when he looks upon his creation and declares it to be good. According to the Sufis, God was a hidden treasure and created human beings because he wanted to be known—that is, wanted new eyes to reflect on the innate perfection and wonder of being.

In welcoming we have the possibility of discovering the same delight, once the separation between the welcomer and what is welcomed, subject and object, falls away and only welcoming, nondual presencing, remains. Our natural state of pure wakefulness reflects reality as it is. It sees no mistakes because it's inseparable from what it sees and has no point of view from which to judge it as adequate or inadequate. Indeed, awareness and its objects are inseparable, and without awareness experience would not be possible. In true welcoming, we are one with the way things are.

Perhaps our sacred role and purpose in this incarnation, as the Sufis suggest, is to bear witness to this precious and irreplaceable moment right now. This is what Nisargadatta Maharaj meant when he said that affectionate awareness is the crucial factor that brings reality into focus and in the process heals all division. Welcoming is the doorway to reality as it is, the nondual. The practice of welcoming naturally elicits heart qualities like love, compassion, gratitude, wonder, and appreciation, because unconditional welcoming is the inherent nature of love itself. In fact, welcoming is the core practice and attitude in the direct approach, an effortless alternative to deliberate mindfulness, and if sustained can take us all the way to nondual realization.

Welcoming Grief, Remorse, and Atonement

Not long ago I was at fault in a minor auto accident in which a cyclist was injured. I watched in horror as he fell off his bike, and I stood over him offering assistance as he lay on the ground clutching his leg in pain. When other people came to help, I withdrew to my car and began shaking uncontrollably as I realized that my carelessness had caused someone else harm despite my deep wish for the benefit of all beings.

Old self-hatred born of a childhood of abuse and abandonment began attacking me as somehow irretrievably flawed and unworthy of love—indeed, unworthy of being at all. Quickly, though, the clouds of shame and self-blame dissipated and I could see the situation from the perspective I bring to just about every other moment of my life—we're not in control of the outcomes in life; the karmic bundle of tendencies and imperfections is not who we really are; and reality unfolds as the inscrutable dance of the mystery, orchestrated by the deep current of love at its heart. Admittedly, it was harder to sustain this view given that I was now the one at fault, and I wanted to welcome all the emotions the incident might evoke rather than try to assert a more awakened perspective.

Over the next few days I continued to welcome my experience as I alternated between long stretches of resting in the awakened view and moments of self-blame, which eventually resolved into waves of grief and remorse. Even though I wasn't in charge at the absolute level and didn't cause harm deliberately, another human being—my brother, my friend, a tender and vulnerable person no different from myself—had been injured, and I was at fault at the relative level. As the grief washed over me, it expanded to include grief for all the ways I had hurt or inconvenienced others over the years, and I found myself drawn to the verse of atonement I used to chant when I was a Zen monk:

> All the twisted karma every committed by me since of old,
> on account of my beginningless greed, hatred, and delusion,
> born of my body, speech, and thought,
> now I atone for it all.

Atonement not in the sense of asking some external authority for forgiveness, but rather of acknowledging the karmic bundle I carry with a combination of acceptance and remorse, returning to at-one-ment with the current of life, and vowing to be more awake and attentive in the future. Sure, I knew, there was no separate someone doing something, but at the relative level I was the person at the wheel of the car, and as a result someone else was hurt. Our mistakes and limitations, no matter how unavoidable, have the power to break the heart open to feel the inevitable pain and grief of being alive in this ephemeral human form where imperfection and loss are our constant companions.

Reflect and Inquire

Spend some time reflecting on how you relate with your experiences, both inner and outer. Do you tend to allow or welcome them just as they are? Or are you constantly alternating between identifying with and attaching to the experiences you like and judging and rejecting the experiences you don't? Sadness is acceptable but anger isn't. Love is great but lust is not. Mindfulness and other forms of awareness meditation train us to be aware of our experience as it is without judgment. But if you look more deeply you may find that awareness itself, without any effort or overlay, already welcomes what is because it's not separate from it. Awareness is already aware—you don't have to do some special practice called mindfulness.

If you're reluctant to welcome and instead keep trying to edit or control your experience, ask yourself why. Are you afraid you may have experiences that make you uncomfortable or challenge the familiar dream self you've cobbled together? Are you trapped in shame or self-judgment and reluctant to welcome your experiences wholeheartedly, especially those that seem negative or unacceptable? Without welcoming, we can't extend love and compassion toward ourselves and will have difficulty welcoming and loving others as well.

Q&A

Q: I've led a life of social action based on my outrage at the inequities and injustices of the status quo. I'm not sure I'm ready to welcome things as they are when they're so bad for so many people—and are getting worse. At the same time, I must admit that my outrage is wearing me out and doesn't seem to be helping, and meditation allows me to relax, at least for a time.

A: Believe it or not, welcoming is a revolutionary act that strikes to the heart of the status quo. The current political and economic order in much of the world is based on dominance and exploitation—of other people and the environment—fueled by greed, aggression, dishonesty, and willful ignorance and disregard. When you rest in awareness and welcome what is, you're relaxing your own tendency to impose your agenda on life and discovering the peace and love that's always available to you whatever the circumstance. Instead of channeling your own aggression to fight back against the powers that be, you're offering a peaceful alternative for yourself and others. No doubt your devotion to social change is fueled by love for those who suffer as well as rage at those that cause their suffering. If you can welcome your adversaries as they are as well, you'll cut through the polarization and conflictual mindset that further fuels the status quo. Of course, welcoming doesn't preclude action of any kind, and you're welcome to continue your social action if you like. But you can do it with an open and welcoming heart rather than outrage.

Q: Several times throughout the book, you critique what you call New Age techniques and teachings and contrast them with the direct approach. Could you explain the similarities and differences? What's wrong with the New Age approach?

A: The term "New Age" is generally used for a philosophy that co-opts nondual or other spiritual truths and uses them in service of the ego and its self-improvement agenda. Yes, we're all one, and everything is interconnected and interdependent. Now how can I use this understanding to manifest my prosperity or improve my health? New Age teachings tend to focus on harnessing universal principles for distinctly individual ends rather than for the good of the whole. This is not necessarily a bad thing to do, of course; sometimes we need special help and healing and this may be the most effective way to get it. But it's not the same as surrendering to the agenda that reality itself in all its mystery has in store.

Also, the New Age inadvertently guilt-trips those who don't get better or manifest more money by suggesting that they're the one in control, rather than the mystery, and their failure is their fault. People who hold to this philosophy may end up feeling like they've failed when life doesn't go their way despite all their practice of New Age techniques. It's not genuine spirituality, just a utilitarian technology based on spiritual principles. The techniques may be effective (or not) at getting what you want, but don't believe the illusion of control the philosophy teaches. You're not in charge, and believing you are is just old-fashioned hubris.

Meditation: Welcoming Difficult Emotions

Intense emotions are especially challenging on the journey of awakening because they tend to hijack our attention and seduce it away from our natural state of openness and ease. This meditation offers an opportunity to investigate the nature of your emotions.

Begin by sitting comfortably and shifting your awareness from your thinking mind to the coming and going of your breath.

As you allow your awareness to open to the full range of sensations throughout your body, notice if you can find any residual negative feelings like anger, sadness, resentment, jealousy, or fear. If you can't sense anything specific, recall a recent difficult event and notice the feelings it evokes. (You can use this meditation with intense positive emotions as well, if they tend to hijack your attention and distract you from being fully present.)

Choose one of the feelings and let your awareness rest there, not with the story, but with the sensations in the body that the feelings evoke. Let go of any images, let go of memories or thoughts that may arise, and just be with the sensations without trying to get rid of them or change them in any way.

Let go of labels like anger, sadness, or fear, which have strong connotations in themselves, and just be with the raw sensations. The clutching in the belly, the pain in the heart, the contraction in the head. Welcome the sensations as they are. Notice any resistance you might have to welcoming the feeling and allow that to be there as well. You're not the feeling; you're the open and welcoming space in which the feeling arises and unfolds.

Now let your awareness fully enter and inhabit the feeling as much as possible. In other words, become the anger, become the sadness, become the fear. Not a separate someone having the emotion, just the emotion itself in all its intensity. This may seem counterintuitive since we usually try to avoid or push away negative feelings. Instead, let the feeling permeate your being without reservation and notice what happens.

Now, shift your awareness to the stories you tell yourself about the feeling, not to indulge them, but merely to become intimate with them. Most negative emotions have a story that generates and perpetuates them. A story about how someone has hurt, wronged, or betrayed you or circumstances have conspired against you. What is the story? Is it familiar? Have you told it before?

Lean into the story or stories and let yourself fall under their spell. How do you react when you believe the story or the stories? What happens to the feeling? Are the stories true? And what price do you pay for believing them?

Now do the opposite. Step back and see them as merely stories, as thoughts your mind generates that may or may not be true. How do you react now? What happens to the feelings? Finally, return to the bare feeling without overlay. Has it shifted or changed in any way? Let it be as it is.

Let go of any effort to be present and just rest as the open, welcoming expanse of awareness itself. Let the feeling unfold in awareness without any further intervention or effort on your part. Let it be just another piece of driftwood afloat on the limitless ocean of awareness. You are the ocean and the emotion is floating in you.

When you feel complete with this meditation, you can get up and go about your day.

8

The Impact of Trauma

As a psychotherapist and spiritual teacher, my understanding of the relationship between trauma and awakening derives not only from my therapy clients and students but from the effect that my own early trauma had on my awakening process. As an infant I was physically abused and abandoned by my mentally ill mother, then adopted by parents who could be loving at times and emotionally and physically abusive at others. Some of the abuse I experienced only came to light after my first major awakening over thirty years ago as I pieced together somatic memories and the reports of others. And some of the earliest and most severe trauma emerged only recently, in the past five to ten years, as post-traumatic stress disorder (PTSD) has become a more commonly used framework for explaining a variety of forms of psychological suffering.

The awakening itself seemed to initiate a process of bringing to the surface shadow parts of my psyche that had only been faintly acknowledged before, as if the influx of the light of awakened awareness drew these parts out of the darkness in search of acknowledgment and release. Over the years, deep inner exploration, supported by the openness and welcoming receptivity of awakened awareness, has helped me to recognize, relate with, and ultimately come to accept and love parts of the psyche that had been rejected in the past and about which I had felt revulsion and shame. Ironically, this very shame and self-blame were feelings that were instilled by the trauma, and it took many years to be able to see and accept them for what they are rather than as the truth of who I am.

I'm writing in some detail about my own trauma here because I want to convey the message that trauma and its effect on our spiritual unfolding is not something we should feel ashamed of—and certainly not something that makes awakening impossible. It's an inextricable part of our karmic bundle over which we have absolutely no control. The best first step in releasing its grip over our lives is to realize how impersonal it is, let go of self-blame and self-judgment, be willing to welcome and allow all the many emotions and parts (see chapter 7), and extend the utmost compassion to ourselves, as we would to someone we love—indeed, because we regard ourselves as someone we love. These are not easy tasks, of course, especially given the sense of worthlessness that so often accompanies complex trauma, but they're worth keeping in mind and heart as we work with trauma on the pathless path.

Perhaps out of a desire to keep the focus firmly on the absolute or transcendent dimension, psychological trauma and the inner complexities that accompany it are rarely addressed in the nondual teachings, past or present, even in our psychologically sophisticated culture. Unfortunately, this tendency to bypass the topic risks emphasizing an unattainable spiritual ideal and marginalizing and even pathologizing the lived experience of so many who arrive on the pathless path desperately seeking understanding, guidance, and support. In our nondual embrace of the full range of human expression, we need to incorporate some insight into the way trauma impacts the awakening process.

Inspired by Rumi, I have been referring to the human psyche as a guesthouse filled with multiple voices, energies, and parts—not a simple system with on or off mode or a centralized command station with one boss in charge, as it's often depicted. This is especially true for those of us who have been traumatized. We host voices and parts that have a particularly strong grip and attempt to exert control because they've experienced times in our lives when our survival was, or appeared to be, at stake, and they felt they had to hold on tight to make it through. This strategy may have protected us at the time of the traumatic event, but later in life the rigidity and resistance to change of these inner parts may cause suffering in various ways and make the letting go required of awakening especially difficult.

Of course, trauma can be a powerful motivator on the path of awakening as well. Those of us who experience PTSD know the profound effect that trauma has had on our lives and may be driven to seek relief from our suffering because it is often so deeply entrenched and resistant to change. On the other hand, we carry a weighty and complex karmic bundle that may slow the awakening and embodiment process and require us to seek help along the way from other modalities like psychological and somatic therapies that directly address and heal the inner divisions caused by the trauma.

Defining Trauma and PTSD

Trauma occurs when you experience an event that seems to threaten your very survival and as a result causes you to feel overwhelmed by shock, confusion, helplessness, fear, and often rage. The term "trauma" doesn't refer to the event itself but to how your body and psyche respond to it. Early studies of of trauma focused on combat veterans who had experienced what used to be called "shell shock," but the term was later generalized to victims of violent crimes, natural disasters, childhood abuse, and other related experiences.

Trauma was originally considered an unusual response to extraordinary events. But ongoing research has shown that it's actually quite common and that your literal survival doesn't have to be at stake for you to be traumatized, as long as you feel that it is. For example, emotional abuse or the loss of a loved one can be traumatic if it seems to threaten your psychological integrity or well-being. Trauma is a subjective experience that depends on your personality and prior experiences and can be mitigated or completely avoided if a trusted figure is there at the time to offer love and support.

According to the psychiatrist Bessel van der Kolk, a pioneer in the study of PTSD, trauma leaves a lasting imprint on the limbic system, a part of the brain focused on survival. Even though the event is long over, the limbic system continues to send messages that you can't relax; you must remain vigilant because your life is in danger. Situations that others might see as benign may cause you to shift into fight-or-flight mode or to freeze and shut down. This complex of reactions is known as PTSD. People with recurring PTSD often have difficulty experiencing pleasure and joy and may suffer from stress-related health problems like high blood pressure or autoimmune disorders.

In practice, psychotherapists often distinguish between several types of trauma. For example, "big-T trauma" results from the classic events that almost inevitably lead to PTSD, such as child physical or sexual abuse, violent crime, sexual assault, life-threatening accidents, and natural disasters. By contrast, "small-t trauma" can be more subtle and subjective. In these cases, whether one has a trauma response will depend on how the event was perceived and the degree of inner resilience and outer support available at the time. Small-t traumas consist of the injuries, losses, disappointments, abandonments, and threats that all of us inevitably encounter in life. Only some of us will experience these as traumatic.

Both big-T and small-t traumas can happen suddenly or unfold over a long period. Single-incident trauma occurs just once and tends to be more amenable to successful resolution. Trauma that occurs repeatedly over an extended period, especially with children, can disrupt normal psychological development. Van der Kolk and other trauma specialists refer to this insidious and long-lasting trauma as developmental trauma, or complex PTSD. Even with a combination of spiritual awakening and intensive psychotherapy, complex PTSD may take a lifetime to resolve. As a psychotherapist and spiritual teacher, I've worked with people who report traumas both great and small, simple and complex, and find that these experiences both enrich and complicate the awakening process.

Pointer: Innate Perfection

One of the principal teachings of the direct approach, shared by Zen, Dzogchen, and Advaita, is that everything is perfect and complete just as it is. Indeed, Dzogchen means "great perfection." But the perfection it points to can't be measured on a relative scale of better or worse, or more or less pristine. Instead, it refers to the essential isness or ineluctable beingness of life as it is. In other words, reality is what it is in all its imperfect completeness and couldn't be otherwise, and this innate perfection is a source of wonder and gratitude. These paradoxical words point not to a concept, but to a direct experience. In the Mahayana tradition this experience is often called "suchness" (*tathata*), the fullness that complements the experience of emptiness. (See the meditation "Innate Perfection" on page 192.)

Even in the midst of the most painful inner conflict, anxiety, depression, or PTSD, you may be able to find at least some momentary peace by flashing on the pristine essential beingness of right now, apart from the worries, concerns, and interpretations your mind imposes on it. Just this! How wondrous and precious! This may be difficult to do at first, but once you break through to this essential level of being you can access it when necessary to free yourself from the dream, at least for a moment, and refresh yourself in the living waters of the ocean of Being.

Why People with Trauma Are Drawn to Awakening

My first Zen teacher used to say monasteries (and by implication ashrams and retreat centers) are places for desperate people—and who could feel more desperate than someone who experiences PTSD on a regular basis? People who have been traumatized are easily overstimulated and emotionally dysregulated and may seek out safe places with minimal stimulation and without potentially threatening interactions. The soothing sounds of the bells and chanting in a monastery or ashram, the predictability of the schedule, the highly stylized and regularized interpersonal relationships, are deeply relaxing and reassuring and provide an antidote to the ongoing inner turmoil and stress of PTSD.

In the Buddhist tradition, the three unavoidable characteristics of human existence are impermanence, insubstantiality, and *dukkha*, usually translated as "suffering" or "dissatisfaction." The Buddhist path to awakening is based on a solution to dukkha known as the four noble truths—the truths of suffering, the cause of suffering, relief from suffering, and the path. Trauma is just an extreme form of dukkha; we're born in the pain of childbirth and go on to a life of inevitable sickness, loss, old age, and death, all of which can be traumatic.

In one of the most famous stories from the early Buddhist scriptures, a woman comes to the Buddha desperately holding her dead baby in her arms and asking for help. The Buddha tells her that he will bring her baby back to life if she can find mustard seeds from the home of a family where no one has died. After desperately searching and being unable to find a single family, she recognizes the inherent nature of loss and grief and has an awakening.

Awakening, then, is the ultimate remedy, the sure heart's release from suffering and trauma. By pointing us away from our identification with the body-mind and the narrative that accompanies it, awakening opens us to our nondual spiritual nature and our true identity with being itself. No wonder that those of us who have experienced more than the usual human allotment of trauma and the extreme contraction and limitation that accompany it would be inexorably drawn to the awakening journey and the boundless openness and freedom it offers. At the same time, trauma and the PTSD that ensues complicate the awakening process in a number of ways and call on us to be especially kind and compassionate with ourselves at every stage of the process.

The Challenge of Waking Up and Staying Awake in the Aftermath of Trauma

In this section I detail some of the core characteristics of trauma and PTSD and how they complicate the awakening process. (In the following section I discuss some of the gifts of trauma on the path.) In some ways, PTSD is the polar opposite of awakening: It strengthens our identification with the narrative rather than freeing us from it, incites fear and hypervigilance rather than trust and ease of being, and elicits feelings of isolation and separation rather than oneness and interconnectedness. Yet it can also heighten our motivation and introduce us to inner strengths and altered states that point the way to waking up. I describe these challenges not to discourage those of you who encounter them, but on the contrary to encourage you to keep going and be especially kind and understanding with yourself.

People who haven't experienced significant trauma often have no idea what the inner life of a traumatized person can be like. It's as if the traumatized have crossed a boundary into an alternate reality that others have never glimpsed and know things are possible that others can't possibly imagine. In my experience and observation, trauma can reveal a dimension of the psyche that harbors a level of fear and danger that only the traumatized recognize because they've been exposed and sensitized to it. As a result, people with trauma may tend to project this darkness out onto the world around them and see it wherever they go, and they may have difficulty opening to and accepting the love that's already available to them.

At the same time, traumatized people may discover the spiritual dimension of reality early in life because their actual circumstances do not provide the love and support they need and they have to turn to more incorporeal sources like spiritual beings or energies or awakened states of mind and heart to supply them. For this reason, they often appear to be old souls who are wiser and more mature than their age-mates as children and who are especially resourceful and resilient as adults.

Likewise, the profound suffering they've experienced tends to make trauma survivors especially empathic and intimately attuned to the suffering of others. This often motivates them not only to seek their own awakening but also to pursue work in the world that helps awaken or heal others or at least benefits them in tangible ways.

Whether or not you suffer from PTSD, however, the fundamental challenges of waking up and staying awake remain more or less the same for us all, and the observations and insights I offer in this section apply to everyone to a greater or lesser degree. As you read through this list, notice which ones resonate and speak to your experience.

Disconnection from Our Essential Nature

As young children, we naturally feel a deep connection with all of life and an ease and trust in the world around us. But repeated abuse or abandonment, especially by those who purportedly love us, may disturb or even shatter this connection and give rise to a sense of being lost, alone, unsafe, and disconnected, not only from others but from our own essential nature. The quest to awaken may be a concerted attempt to recapture the sense of connection we've lost. Alternatively, trauma may cause us to seek connection in a more spiritual or incorporeal dimension of existence.

Pointer: Beyond Trauma

Remember, no matter how blissful or disturbing, pleasurable or painful, desirable or undesirable may be the thoughts, memories, and emotions you experience, "you" can't be found there. Instead, you abide as the experiencer prior to all experience, the context behind all content–inherently open, peaceful, loving, and undisturbed. Who you really are is beyond all trauma. Let your true nature shine forth like the sun and invite a lifetime of PTSD to be released from the shadows. In the end, the painful thoughts and memories don't define you. Let love and awakened awareness prevail!

Difficulty Disengaging and Disidentifying from Content

Most of us have difficulty seeing our beliefs, stories, thoughts, emotions, and memories as just contents of awareness rather than as the truth of who we are. But disidentifying from thoughts and emotion can be much more challenging when those contents of mind and body are insisting, without a shadow of a doubt, that your life is in danger and you need to immediately flee or protect yourself or you'll die. Because these signals are based on a primitive nervous-system response, they tend to hijack awareness and make disidentification difficult if not impossible.

Fear of Annihilation

Trauma in childhood may cause us to feel that we're not safely contained and supported by life, and may give rise to a sense of inner chaos and fragmentation. As a result, glimpses of the boundaryless openness of awakened awareness and the essential emptiness of the manifest world—insights we may have been actively seeking—may seem to threaten us with the disintegration and annihilation we feared as children. After my own first major awakening, which occurred quite unexpectedly, I alternated between extended periods of profound stillness and peace and moments of terror at the groundless ground that had opened beneath me.

Conflicting Intentions and Agenda

As humans we're complex creatures, with multiple inner parts and subpersonalities (see chapter 7). But people who experienced developmental trauma as children often host parts that are especially disconnected and out of touch with one another, with a cacophony of voices that reflect the chaos of our family of origin. For example, one part may desperately want to awaken, while another is terrified of letting go, another rebels against authority, and another holds crippling self-doubt.

These conflicting intentions and agendas can complicate the journey of awakening in understandable ways. Once awakening occurs, the recognition that there's no single separate self in charge may allow the parts more freedom to interact and find a more natural inner balance and harmony. Or it can elicit fear and intensify the inner turmoil. At the same time, this complexity of parts may express itself as enhanced creativity and freedom from limiting structures of thought and expression.

Distorted Worldview

If we learned through early trauma that the world is a threatening and unsafe place, we may have a tendency to expect the worst and anticipate catastrophe around every corner. As a result, we'll find it more difficult than most people to let go of our compulsive planning and strategizing and realize the innate perfection of each moment. If we felt separate, alone, and unloved as children, we won't be able to relax as easily into the nondual field and experience our oneness with all of life.

Emotional Hijacking and Hyperarousal

Because trauma leaves a lasting imprint on the limbic system in the brain, it continues to send messages that you can't relax but must remain hypervigilant because your life is in danger. Situations that others might see as benign—even sitting alone on a meditation cushion—can hijack your inner life and cause you to shift into fight-or-flight mode or to freeze and shut down. This makes it especially challenging to simply be present without reactivity and welcome reality just as it is.

Obsessive Thinking, Rigid Thought Patterns, and Resistance to Change

The threat of inner chaos and emotional overwhelm in the aftermath of trauma may give rise to obsessive thought patterns that seem to offer an illusion of control and stability but also make it difficult to open and to let go of the beliefs and stories that dominate the inner life. Attachment to this illusion can cause you to hold on tight to familiar habits of thought and behavior even when they don't contribute to your well-being or serve your awakening.

Confusing No-Self with De-Selfing

Abused children are often forced to relinquish their sense of agency and autonomy and succumb to the control of the abuser, in a process psychologists call "de-selfing." By contrast, realizing no self—that is, seeing through the illusion of a single separate self in charge—enhances our freedom and autonomy while at the same time inviting us to surrender to a reliable order beneath the uncertainty and constant change. In de-selfing you end up feeling worthless, frozen, and bound by shame and guilt. In realizing no self, you experience yourself as having innate autonomy and value. If you confuse no self with the de-selfing you experienced in childhood, you may understandably consider awakening an unattractive or frightening prospect.

Emotional Flooding Caused by the Easing of Repression

Repression is the psychological mechanism by which some thoughts, emotions, impulses, and memories are automatically shunted out of conscious awareness into the shadows of the psyche (often called "the unconscious" in Western psychology). Awakening tends to reverse this process, and the repressed contents may flood into awareness at unexpected times. If these contents are traumatic, they can feel overwhelming and retrigger the trauma.

Dissociation, Pro and Con

Besides repression, the other predominant way the psyche protects itself from trauma is through a process known as dissociation. Instead of experiencing the event in the moment and then hiding the memory and emotions in the shadows, as in repression, we shift into an altered state that allows us to avoid the experience in the moment itself. For example, you may imagine yourself on the ceiling or disappear into a fantasy inner life or do math problems in your head while the traumatic event is taking place.

This ability to state-shift may cause spiritual states to be more readily available and make the shift into nondual awareness easier later in life. It may also have the spiritual benefit of causing us to question conventional reality and seek a deeper understanding. At the same time, however, it may make it more difficult to remain present to our experience from moment to moment in ordinary life.

Lack of Essential Inner Structures That Stabilize the Psyche

Developmental psychology in the West teaches that healthy bonding and "good-enough" parenting as a child help us develop inner psychic structures that make happy, well-adjusted functioning possible as an adult. Without them, some psychologists suggest, it's very difficult if not impossible to let go of control and trust the natural order that takes care of life without effort on our part.

One twentieth-century Zen master in the tradition I studied for many years claimed that Zen was only for people in excellent mental health. The Buddhist psychologist Jack Engler similarly said that you have to be somebody before you can be nobody. Both statements suggest that you need the ability to function well enough and stay focused long enough to engage with the teachings and practices necessary for awakening.

In my experience, awakening seems to occur whether or not these developmental milestones have been fully met and these inner structures firmly established. But functioning from an awakened perspective in their absence may be more challenging, as the conflicting emotions and impulses they guard against exert greater influence over our behavior. In the end, these psychic structures can be elusive and difficult to find or measure, since they have no material existence and only exist as the hypotheses of certain psychological theories.

Pointer: The Dark Inside the Light

One of the unexpected complexities of the awakening journey is that the more you open to the love, light, clarity, emptiness, and purity of your essential nature, the more you invite the darker energies of fear, hatred, confusion, and aggression that lurk in the shadows to rush to the surface to be seen and released into the light. For example, long-repressed traumatic memories may flood into conscious awareness unbidden and you may feel overwhelmed with painful and unresolved past emotions that demand your immediate attention. The more awake you become, the more you may feel you're being pulled down into the dark, and you may conclude that you're doing something wrong and have lost your way.

In reality, this is a common and often unavoidable part of waking up. The radical openness of awakened awareness, coupled with a commitment to truth at every level, tend to break down the walls and barriers in the psyche that have divided one part from the other, in a natural movement toward greater wholeness and integration. Just continue your practices of inquiry and effortless mindfulness and welcome these experiences as they arise. Eventually you'll get used to the process and the difficult and seemingly antithetical experiences will naturally resolve and integrate. If you feel overwhelmed and need assistance, don't hesitate to seek the guidance of a psychotherapist or spiritual teacher who has some understanding of the complexities of spiritual experience.

Allegiance to Suffering

People with trauma tend to expect and even invite similar trauma later in life by making unwise choices and gravitating to people and situations that resemble their abuser and the abuse they experienced. (Freud called this tendency the "repetition compulsion.") On their awakening journey, they may be especially attached to entrenched negative beliefs about self and other and have difficulty letting go of old patterns of behavior that no longer serve them well.

Working with Trauma on the Path of Awakening

Because of my own experiences growing up, I specialized in trauma in my work as a therapist and had the good fortune to study with the originator of one of the most effective trauma release techniques, eye movement desensitization and reprocessing (EMDR). Over the years I helped many people who had struggled their entire adult lives with their PTSD, and the accompanying anxiety and depression, to begin to chip away at the burden they carried. In some cases, they were able to step across a threshold into a new level of freedom and joy. Notice that

I didn't say they released their trauma entirely; in my experience most of us who were traumatized early continue to carry some of the scars—the reactivity, the proclivity toward anxiety or depression, the physical ailments—throughout our lives. But once we discover our natural state of awakened awareness, we spend more and more time in openness and ease of being and less and less in suffering and identification.

Post-traumatic stress centers on an imaginary, separate self that's based in the body-mind and feels endangered long after the traumatic event is over. Trauma intensifies and fixates this identification and makes seeing through the illusion of the self especially difficult. At the same time, of course, the most potent antidote and source of healing for the trauma is precisely the recognition that the separate self that's apparently threatened doesn't exist and has never existed, and that the past is over and only exists as a story in the present. The ongoing process of healing trauma post-awakening involves deepening and embodying this recognition. Ironically, however, this recognition may trigger fear in those who have felt in the past that their lives were at stake, because "no self" may be confused in the nervous system with the annihilation of self. Such are the complexities of PTSD.

Integrate, Assimilate, and Apply Nondual Realization as the Ultimate Medicine for Trauma

Here's an example from my own experience of how this integration and healing may occur. I had awakened to the nondual nature of reality and deeply recognized that inside and outside, self and other, subject and object, are just expressions of the boundless and seamless nondual field. Yet there were still moments when the traumatized child in my psyche would contract in fear of the imagined dangers outside myself. Then one day when this child part was available and more open than usual, it was able to receive the message deep in the core of my being that there is no outside to be afraid of—just this single, undivided being that I am. Suddenly the child relaxed as never before and the burden of fear lifted.

This visceral recognition can't be orchestrated by the conscious mind that easily grasps such truths; it needs to dawn in its own mysterious and inimitable way so that it registers deeply and transforms the reactivity in the body and nervous system, where it's been imprinted. This process may need to happen repeatedly, as the awakened understanding penetrates deeper and deeper into the shadows of the lower chakras and more primitive parts of the brain. It can't be rushed and requires unlimited patience and compassion for the vulnerable, frightened, traumatized parts of ourselves. These are some of the infinite, endless awakenings I refer to in the title of this book.

If you haven't awakened yet and don't have any nondual realization to integrate and assimilate, you can still enlist skillful means and methods like the following for working with trauma on the awakening journey:

Connect with Self-Love and Self-Compassion

People who have experienced complex trauma tend to harbor the belief that they're inadequate or worthless and undeserving of love and support. This belief makes connecting with their inherent self-love especially challenging, but also especially necessary. They may need to repeatedly renew this connection as an ongoing antidote to the trauma and the dark forces of self-attack that were unleashed and continue to operate beneath the surface—or, in neuroscience terms, to quell the constant reactivation of the primitive limbic and reptilian parts of the brain.

For this purpose, I recommend traditional practices like metta (loving-kindness) and tonglen (taking and sending) from the Buddhist tradition, examples of which are readily available in books or on the internet. (For a brief metta meditation, see page 55.) Once you're able to offer this love and compassion to yourself, you can internalize it as an ongoing part or function of your psyche that mirrors the natural love of consciousness or awareness for its expressions in form and continues to welcome your experience just as it is (see chapter 7). Remember, you are this love, you don't have to manufacture it from scratch or seek it outside yourself. You have difficulty accessing it only because of your trauma, as well as our ordinary human tendency to be hard on ourselves.[1]

Listen to, Reassure, and Love the Traumatized Parts

Once you've established this welcoming and loving function or part of the psyche, you can engage in the ongoing practice of welcoming the traumatized parts and the painful emotions and memories they carry into conscious awareness with love and compassion. Awakening in its early stages may be dry and impersonal and lack the heart dimension that the traumatized parts need. Insight into the limitless, groundless nature of reality may not reassure those primitive places that seek a more visceral, heartfelt, earthbound sense of security and support. They want to hear words like "I love you. I'm here for you. You're safe now" rather than "the separate self is an illusion" or "reality is empty of substantiality." In fact, they may experience the emphasis on groundlessness or emptiness as frightening, repugnant, and unwanted until they've established an ongoing felt-sense of safety and love.

Remember, Recognize, Return, and Rest in Awareness on a Regular Basis

Once you've realized your natural state of inherent wakefulness, the best way to integrate it into your life is to keep returning to it throughout the day and rest there, in a practice I call the four Rs: remember, recognize, return, and rest. For those who have been traumatized, this resting can become a refuge from the reactive emotions and intrusive memories that keep arising even after awakening has occurred. Essentially, the practice is to keep returning to who you really are when you forget and begin to identify with the traumatized parts. *Remember* that this reactivity is not a reflection of who you really are, stop and *recognize* your natural state, come home and *rest* there, and keep *returning* when you get caught up again.

Hang Out in the Light

As an antidote to the darkness that the trauma has imprinted in the psyche, those of us who have been traumatized can keep returning to bask in the limitless love and light that awakening reveals at the heart of existence. Some traditions recommend visualizing this love and light in your own heart and radiating it out through the body and beyond in every direction. In the same spirit, you might want to avoid negativity and focus instead on more positive possibilities in every aspect of your life—for example, by emphasizing harmony in your personal relationships and gravitating to uplifting media content rather than the stories of violence and devastation that fill newspapers, TV, and movies.

Do Whatever You Can to Minimize Ongoing Stress and Avoid Further Trauma and Limbic System Reactivation.

Though ongoing meditation may not be necessary to wake up or stay awake, it's uniquely effective in calming the nervous system, easing anxiety, and releasing negative or depressive thought patterns. Again, these are progressive practices that can be very helpful in working with and even healing trauma both pre- and post-awakening. People with trauma are often accustomed—and sometimes even addicted—to living with ongoing stress and may feel restless and unfulfilled if they don't get their daily dose of adrenaline. It may take years to get used to a more relaxed way of life.

Find Refuge in Sangha

Seek out others on the awakening journey who have experienced significant trauma and feel free to speak openly about it and its impact on your awakening process. Sharing your experience with like-minded people tends to release the burden of carrying it on your own and creates a supportive sense of community. Some people who come from addictive families find twelve-step groups helpful, even if they don't have addiction issues themselves.

Accept That the Trauma May Never Be Fully Resolved and Love Yourself Anyway

Here again, self-compassion is crucial. Despite our aspiration to achieve abiding enlightenment and freedom from suffering, we're imperfect creatures who can make only limited changes to the karmic bundle we were handed. In any case, we're not in charge and have no control over what gets transformed and released. In "Verses on the Faith Mind" the Third Patriarch Seng Ts'an teaches that to be enlightened is not to be perfect, but to be without anxiety about imperfection. Or to paraphrase the longtime Zen practitioner Leonard Cohen, there's a crack in everything, that's where the light gets in.

Work with a Professional Trauma Therapist

Finally, don't hesitate to work with an experienced trauma therapist or healer because you think it's somehow unspiritual. Awakening and healing are parallel tracks that run side by side and inform and empower each other. Since trauma is often so deeply ingrained in the body and nervous system, it's best to find a therapist who incorporates one or more somatic techniques, such as EMDR, brainspotting, or somatic experiencing, and has extensive experience applying them with a range of different clients and kinds of trauma. Some familiarity with the benefits of meditation and spiritual awakening would also be helpful, if not essential.

Reflect and Inquire

Before you begin to reflect, remember that thoughts of past trauma can trigger flashbacks and other symptoms of PTSD. If you feel comfortable moving forward, spend some time reflecting on the trauma you've experienced, whether in childhood or as an adult.

Have you ever considered the possibility that certain experiences in your life had a traumatic impact? You may have experienced a single-incident or small-t trauma like the loss of a pet or being embarrassed in front of your friends. Or you may have endured repeated physical, sexual, or emotional abuse as a child. How do you think these traumatic experiences continue to affect your life now? Do you find yourself becoming agitated or afraid for no apparent reason in certain situations? Do your emotional reactions sometimes seem out of proportion to the situation at hand?

On your journey of awakening, have you felt that this reactivity and the other signs of PTSD outlined in this chapter have affected your ability to realize your true nature and live from your deeper understanding in everyday life? Do any of the challenges described have particular resonance for you? On the other hand, how has your experience of trauma motivated you in your search for a deeper source of happiness and peace of mind and heart? Have these traumatic experiences worked to your advantage in any way when it comes to awakening? What have you done—and what else could you be doing—to address the trauma at a psychological level?

Q&A

Q: You say that "the best first step in releasing trauma's grip over our lives is to realize how impersonal it is, let go of self-blame and self-judgment, be willing to welcome and allow all the many parts of ourselves, and extend the utmost compassion to ourselves, as we would to someone we love." How can we do this on a practical level? I believe acceptance must come from the heart, not just the head, but I find it difficult to do in an honest and authentic way.

A: Ultimately the resolution of trauma happens in the heart and nervous system, but a conceptual understanding of where the trauma comes from and how it affects us is a crucial first step. We need to understand that it wasn't our fault and has nothing to do with who we really are. Hearing this repeatedly from people we trust, like spiritual teachers, therapists, and trauma experts, can go a long way to releasing the grip of shame and blame.

At a day-to-day level, the regular practice of some form of awareness meditation, such as the effortless mindfulness described in this book, guides us in inviting the traumatic feelings into conscious awareness and welcoming them with kindness and without shame. At an even deeper level, realizing directly for ourselves that our true nature is inherently pure, unconditioned, and free of the dream narrative we've woven about our lives can loosen the grip even further. In the end, though, most people who continue to experience the aftereffects of trauma will need the help of professionals who specialize in trauma healing.

Q: You discuss how trauma can make disidentification from the story of self particularly difficult. I have found this to be the case. Each step in my process has required self-work prior to each depth of realization. In your experience, is there a threshold of healing required before awakening can be fully embodied, or can awakening itself be leveraged as part of the trauma healing process?

A: In my own experience and my work with students, I've found that it's possible to wake up out of the narrative in a heartbeat, no matter how painful the narrative may be, and glimpse our true nature free of trauma and identification. Once experienced, this recognition has a powerful healing effect in its own right. But trauma tends to hijack the nervous system and make it difficult to live from the awakening on an ongoing basis because it's so deeply programmed in the survival centers of the brain like the limbic system and so-called reptilian brain.

As far as I can tell, there's no particular threshold of healing required for the next stage in your awakening; it differs from person to person. I recommend trusting your own judgment about when therapeutic help is needed, and as always extend to yourself the same kindness, compassion, and respect you would to any other person you love, which itself can be profoundly healing. For this I recommend traditional practices like metta (loving-kindness) and tonglen (taking and sending). Those of us who have been traumatized are often especially hard on ourselves and particularly in need of such loving attention.

Meditation: Innate Perfection

Beyond dualities like perfect and imperfect lies the irreducible beingness of life as it is, which is perfectly orchestrated in some mysterious way beyond our mind's comprehension. Rarely do we stop and appreciate this perfect orchestration that sustains our individual lives in countless ways.

Begin by sitting quietly and allowing your body to settle. Take a few deep breaths and rest in awareness.

Now become aware of the coming and going of your breath, the inhalation and the exhalation. Notice how breathing happens on its own, without any thinking, planning, or effort on your part. In fact, if you try to breathe, you just interfere with the natural rhythm that's already taking place.

Be aware of your heart—how it beats on its own, regularly, naturally, and effortlessly, sending blood, oxygen, and nutrients throughout your body. It doesn't require any deliberation or planning on your part. Any attempt to control it would be a waste of time and energy.

Consider all your internal organs—your stomach and intestines, your liver and pancreas, your endocrine glands, your brain. They do the intricate, complex work of keeping you alive and healthy without any thought or effort on your part.

How amazing! What a priceless gift! You didn't have to do anything to deserve this gift, yet it's been handed to you, your birthright as a human being.

Now turn your awareness outward and consider the air you breathe. It's been gifted to you free of charge, and it comes to your nostrils and lips and lungs unbidden, without any effort. Breathing in, breathing out—the most natural activity in the world—and you rarely notice or appreciate it unless for some reason your breathing is impeded in some way.

The same with the sky, the ground, the sun, the water—free of charge, your birthright as a human being here on Earth. Notice what emotions these reflections evoke.

Consider how perfectly matched your body and your senses are with the experiences they encounter. How the food you eat is perfectly designed to taste good in your mouth and provide your body the nutrients it needs. How the green of the grass and trees, and the blue of the sky and water, soothe and nourish your heart and mind. How your ears are suited to hear the natural sounds of the wind and the birds, and your fingers to feel the textures of the earth, the delicacy of a flower petal, the bark of a tree, the hands of a friend.

Everything in your life has been perfectly designed to work together in harmony to allow you to continue living as you do. Otherwise, you wouldn't be here, listening to these words.

Certainly, as the mind may be quick to remind you, there are challenges and difficulties, failures and losses, sickness and death. Certainly there are people who don't have clean water and air and good food, as you do. Certainly human beings are threatening the delicate balance of nature that has sustained our species for many thousands of years, and you may feel moved to do whatever you can to improve these situations.

But right now, there is a perfectly orchestrated interconnectedness that makes this precious moment possible. You don't need to believe in a God to acknowledge the exquisite and intricate intelligence that guides your life from moment to moment.

Spend some time contemplating this innate harmony and interconnectedness. Notice how this contemplation affects you, the feelings of wonder and appreciation and gratitude it may evoke. When you feel complete for now, feel free to get up and go about your day.

9

Awakening Relationship

In everyday conversation, when we speak of relationships we're generally referring to the complex network of intimate interactions and connections we have with friends, family members, and significant others that provide support, meaning, and context to our lives. Without such vital interpersonal ties, we would not be able to survive as vulnerable human beings in a world of forces beyond our control.

Because they're so essential to our survival and encoded in our biology, such core relationships are fraught with powerful emotions and informed by a lifetime of conditioning and experience. Ask anyone who has ever experienced a divorce or the loss of a loved one—or anyone who has been traumatized by a family member, as I discuss in the previous chapter. The powerful energies of love and attachment provide us with a precious opportunity to practice staying in alignment with our deepest realization in emotionally challenging situations—and to apply, integrate, and embody our spiritual understanding in everyday life. For this reason, intimate relationship can be engaged as a spiritual path unto itself.

But relationship in its most elemental sense—that is, the ways we relate with our ongoing experience, both inner and outer—has even more fundamental importance and lies at the heart of the awakening journey. If we're identified with our thoughts and feelings and resisting or struggling against life as it is, we're relating in a way that causes suffering to ourselves and others. When we wake up out of our identification with the contents of our experience and recognize our deeper identity as the boundless awareness or space in which experience arises and life unfolds, this more awakened relationship frees us from the story of our lives and opens us to a new level of happiness and peace of mind. (See chapter 6, page 119.) In the metaphor of the guesthouse from Rumi's poem in chapter 7, our relationship with our experience shifts from being lost and confused among the throng of guests to being the host who welcomes, honors, and entertains even the most troublesome visitors while not becoming involved in the drama they promote.

In the most profound level of relationship, nondual realization, the ordinary parameters of relationship are transcended and subject and object, self and other, inside and outside are realized to be not separate but rather simply aspects or facets of an indivisible totality. No separate experiencer, nothing separate experienced; only experiencing, only pure presence. In this nonrelationship, the sense of a separate self falls away, the distinction between inside and outside dissolves, and "just this" remains—the nondual field, being, or consciousness itself, beyond the divisions the mind projects. Though this deepest level of relating may be glimpsed only fleetingly in its clarity and fullness, it can continue to inspire and transform the ways we relate in ordinary life.

At this deepest level of reality, there is no separate self, there are no separate things, there's only relationship, only interrelatedness, one vast and inextricable web of interbeing—and love is the energy that animates and infuses it. In Zen this nonseparation is sometimes called "intimacy with all things" and is considered the hallmark and fruition of spiritual realization. Sitting beside a mountain stream, we may find the apparent separation between water, rock, and flesh and blood dissolving into the living present—just mountain, just stream, just this. Indeed, what evolves as we awaken is precisely our relationship with our experience as we go from being identified with the dream of separation, to recognizing that we are the awake awareness or consciousness that welcomes all experience just as it is, to realizing the inseparability of inside and outside, subject and object, experiencer and experienced, self and other in the nondual field. At its foundation, the pathless path that draws us inexorably onward is a journey of deepening relationship that culminates in the realization of our inherent inseparability—instead of one-to-one relationship, we have interbeing, nonduality, not two.

Spiritual practice and self-inquiry guide us to question the nature of relationship at the deepest level. When we ask, "Who or what am I?" we're inquiring into one pole of the dualistic relationship of subject and object—an apparent "I" in here and "other" out there—in the hope that the question will dissolve in a deeper insight into the nondual nature of what is. Relationship is the context in which this inquiry takes place. Who or what is the self, and what is it in relationship with? This is the core question on the awakening journey. How do we relate with life as it unfolds? Do we struggle and resist, or do we welcome what is?

Both this chapter and chapter 7, "Welcoming What Is," are about living in relationship from our awakened understanding moment after moment in everyday life. This process is known as spiritual embodiment or integration, the maturity to apply our insights into the nature of reality to our ongoing relationship with life itself. If our realization is limited to certain moments in meditation or self-inquiry and doesn't transpose into ongoing intimacy with actual people and situations, it has little practical value.

Our intimate relationships are a microcosm of our relationships more broadly, and as a result provide an invaluable laboratory in which to experiment with embodying and expressing our awakened understanding. Can I remain openhearted, loving, surrendered, and nonreactive with the people closest to me? Can I stay awake to our inseparability in the presence of intense emotions and habitual patterns? Can I communicate in ways that foster greater love and togetherness rather than conflict and division? And when I can't, how can I bring my deepest realization to bear to guide me home to awakened relating? As it goes in intimate relationships, so it follows in our relationships more broadly with the world inside and around us.

Not surprisingly, intimate romantic relationships are an especially challenging proving ground because they generally involve at least two dimensions of love that may pull us in different directions: pure, unconditional love, which arises spontaneously without external cause, expressing itself through the heart and the upper chakras as a radiant light that shines forth into the world like the sun, and instinctual, embodied love, or eros, which expresses itself through the heart and lower chakras and drives human attachment and sexual connection. Pure love inspires us to extend empathy, compassion, generosity, gratitude, and appreciation without requiring anything in return; eros draws us to connect in visceral ways that provide pleasure and fulfillment at a more embodied experiential level but may trigger powerful reactive emotions if it's not reciprocated. In the nondual spiritual traditions, unconditional love free of attachment is held up as the highest ideal, while eros has been considered problematic and antithetical to the path of awakening, except in the traditions of nondual tantra. Understandably, the mixture of the two in a single relationship can prove emotionally charged and especially difficult to negotiate.

Perfect Love, Imperfect Relationships

As an emotion, love arises in the human heart in countless guises—appreciation, gratitude, compassion, caring, loving-kindness, empathy, equanimity, interconnectedness—and expresses itself in different relationships in various forms. But in its essence, love is more than just an emotion—it's a universal energy and intelligence that underlies the workings of the universe and can provide a reliable guidance system for our lives, as when we check in with the intuition of the heart to determine how to act. (In fact, the heart appears to have a nervous system akin to the one centered in the brain that generates its own form of heart-centered knowing.[1])

At the deepest level, love is what we are fundamentally—the light of consciousness that pervades and illuminates all experience, the sacred energy that holds reality together and fuels the manifest world, beyond the differences of this and that, loving or unloving. This essential nature of love spontaneously comes to the foreground and can be felt in the heart when we abide in our natural state of nondual presence.

In the Tibetan tradition, this pure love is known as *bodhichitta* (literally, "awakened heart-mind"), the deep wish for the benefit of all beings without regard for the needs of the separate self. Bodhichitta functions both as a quality we can cultivate or directly recognize as our natural state (relative bodhichitta) and as a fundamental principle or aspect of reality itself (absolute bodhichitta). As its name implies, bodhichitta is the energy that motivates the activities of bodhisattvas (awakened beings), who put the awakening of all beings ahead of their own. In the Mahayana Buddhist tradition, love, as compassion, is the flip side of wisdom—insight into the empty and insubstantial nature of reality and the four noble truths of suffering give rise to love, and love for all beings (bodhichitta) gives rise to the deeper nondual wisdom of our interbeing and inseparability.

In Advaita Vedanta, love and wisdom are likewise experienced as inseparable. There is the saying, attributed to Nisargadatta Maharaj: "When I look within and see that I am nothing, there is wisdom. When I look without and see that I am everything, there is love. Between these two my life flows." In Vedanta in general, the fundamental nature of reality is considered to be *satchitananda*, "being-consciousness-bliss," with ananda—usually translated as bliss, joy, or delight—being an essential form of love. When we find joy in seeing a beautiful sunset or delight in the face of a loved one, we are experiencing love without condition or reservation. Such love or joy can arise in any moment as we contemplate the innate beauty and perfection of what is, no matter how it presents itself.

Such moments of unconditional love or joy without apparent external cause may motivate us to find ways of experiencing it more often and to seek the deeper and more abiding source of love within, in our true nature, the universal heart we share. This core motivation fuels the journey of spiritual awakening. When we search for such abiding and perfect love in the imperfect form of human relationships, however, problems inevitably arise because, like all manifest reality, such relationships are uncertain, unreliable, constantly changing, and inherently empty of substantiality. Yet search we do, and have done since time immemorial, driven by forces beyond our control.

For Western psychologists these forces may include the tendency to project our best and most appealing qualities onto the idealized other and seek them there (Jung); the power of our early survival-level attachment to the mother or other caring, nurturing figures that draws us back again and again to reenact the primal bond with a significant other (attachment theorists); and the primordial energy of eros that seeks union with another in order to satisfy deep-seated instinctual desires and perpetuate the species (Freud and his followers). In the devotional traditions, this energy of love is channeled into love for the divine beloved, often embodied in a particular deity or archetype. Ultimately, love is a divine power and force far greater than the individual; it is not just an emotion we experience, but a power that we can become a greater vehicle or vessel to express. Where love is, I am not.

As long as we seek the abiding source of love outside ourselves, we'll be frustrated and unfulfilled for a number of reasons. For one thing, the love of another can never consistently provide precisely the love, nurturing, caring, and support we seek moment to moment at a personal level. For another, as we come to realize the profound beauty, intelligence, and sacred perfection of the love that we inherently are, we find that we are unable to embody and express it with another in a consistently kind, tender, skillful, and caring way. Yet the purity and luminosity of this perfect love continues to inspire the heart to keep trying to give and receive it, no matter how flawed and imperfect our attempts may inevitably be. This process of inspiration, aspiration, and disappointment fuels the journey of awakened relationships.

In the end, we need to acknowledge that relationships in this imperfect human realm will inevitably be imperfect, no matter how pure the love, and any attempt to hold ourselves to some spiritual ideal is destined to cause more suffering. In fact, this very welcoming of our imperfection is one of the hallmarks of awakened living. In the words of the Third Patriarch, from his "Verses on the Faith Mind," to be enlightened "is not to worry about perfection or non-perfection," including, of course, in the arena of intimate relationships.[2]

Pointer: The Trap of Perfectionism

Even though they're often cautioned against striving to achieve some special state, many people bring their competitiveness and goal-oriented approach to the pathless path and struggle to live up to some spiritual ideal. In fact, given the variety of nondual teachings in the spiritual marketplace these days, seekers may read multiple books with different orientations—Zen, Dzogchen, Advaita, New Age, neo-Advaita—and try to emulate them all. The problem is, imitation may be the highest form of flattery but it's not realization. Every genuine awakening has its own unique qualities and trajectory, and yours may look nothing like the Buddha's or Ramana Maharshi's.

Many of the teachings about what constitutes perfect and abiding realization come from teachers and sages who lived as renunciant monks or yogis and did not have to face the challenges and complexities of making a living or raising a family in the twenty-first century. For example, you may be confronted with reactive emotions and relationship issues that they never encountered in the ashram or monastery, and as a result your post-awakening journey may be far more tumultuous and unpredictable than theirs.

I encourage you to stop evaluating and judging your progress according to some imagined standard and rest in the ineffable mystery of the present moment. As I wrote after a retreat many years ago:

> The mind is constantly trying to figure out
> what page it's on in the story of itself.
> Close the book. Burn the bookmark.
> End of story. Now the dancing begins.

Aspire to realize perfect and abiding awakening, if you like, but at the same time welcome yourself and your karmic bundle as is. As my first Zen teacher, Shunryu Suzuki, used to say, you're constantly losing your balance against a background of perfect balance.

The Promise and Challenge of Eros

Intimate romantic relationships are the stuff of popular movies and songs for a reason: They resonate deeply with our heart's desire to find happiness, pleasure, and mutual fulfillment in the arms of a life partner who shares our outlook on life and our desires for an ongoing, meaningful connection, often involving family, children, and broader relationships with the community or tribe at large. Monogamous lifelong connections of this kind seem to be hardwired in our human genome, and eros is the energy that drives and informs them.

However, such relationships can never provide us with the perfectly attuned love and connection we crave, because we're inherently imperfect expressions of the pure and unconditional love we know ourselves to be. This imperfection is inevitable. As long as we live in a dream narrative of our own devising, with an illusory separate self at the center, we can't love unconditionally because we experience life through the filter of "me" and "mine" and all the conditioning and trauma we've accumulated in this human incarnation. And as long as we're focusing primarily on our own needs, we only have so much love and energy available to give to others. Despite these unavoidable imperfections, however, we continue to long for perfect connection, especially in the realm of eros, where the desire for intimacy at the emotional and often sexual level can be so intense.

What exactly is eros, and why does it exert such a powerful hold over our lives? In the most limited sense, eros is the desire for sexual satisfaction, with or without the higher energies of love, driven by the instinctual urge to procreate and perpetuate the species. In a more universal sense, as Western psychologists like Freud and Jung have pointed out, eros is love expressing itself as the life force, the energy that connects us with other beings and the world around us. Eros is the drive that brings lovers together, and it's also the tie that binds mother and child or causes a father to sacrifice his life for his offspring. These familial—and by extension tribal—relationships are forged in the fire of eros and have a powerful tenacity because eros holds them together.

More broadly still, eros is the life energy that courses through the body and through reality itself, and it's the passion and love of life that draws us into the world rather than out of it, keeping us engaged. In the tradition of nondual Shaiva tantra, eros is Shakti, the divine feminine energy or principle of birthing, becoming, manifestation, diversity—the endless dance or flow of life. Shakti is in eternal union with Shiva, the universal masculine energy of the principle of oneness, Being, stillness, wisdom, transcendence. This union of Shiva and Shakti represents the balance and equipoise at the heart of life in its mysterious unfolding.

Primal and instinctual though it is, eros experienced at the interpersonal level also has a sacred dimension because it offers us a unique opportunity to dissolve the boundaries between self and other, unite the opposites, merge with another human being, and achieve blissful union with life itself—something that's otherwise only offered in nondual and mystical spiritual traditions. Like spiritual awakening, eros promises the death of separation in our collective interconnectedness or interbeing, with the act of sexual union experienced as a kind of sacrifice for the species and for life itself. Hence the allure of eros is the allure of self-surrender, and so channels the same longing for union that drives us to awaken.

Here, for example, is an excerpt from an article I wrote for *Tricycle* magazine on how eros sometimes goes astray and expresses itself through sexual relationships between spiritual teachers and their students:

> Among the earthly pleasures available to us, sex is arguably the one that most closely resembles the spiritual illumination to which we as spiritual seekers aspire. In moments of deep sexual union with our beloved, we're granted an opportunity to dissolve our physical and energetic boundaries and enter a selfless, timeless, boundaryless realm where we feel deeply connected, even merged, with all of life. In the fleeting ecstasy of orgasm, we may catch a glimpse of the transcendent bliss that often accompanies the enlightenment experience. And in the feelings of tranquility and satisfaction that follow, we may find echoes of the peace and completeness that are characteristics of our essential spiritual nature. In fact, sex for some people can be a powerful doorway to spiritual illumination.
>
> On a more instinctual level, of course, sex grips us with unparalleled urgency precisely because it rules our lower energy centers and is inextricably linked to the survival of the species. Without sex, quite simply, we would not be. Powerful hormones governed by the more primitive parts of the brain drive us to procreate whether or not our neocortex agrees. In the earliest teachings attributed to the Buddha, sex is regarded as the chief expression of the craving or thirst that gives rise to attachment and suffering and propels us forward relentlessly on the wheel of samsara. In the thrall of sexual desire, after all, we human beings have been known to behave in some remarkably impulsive, irrational, and irresponsible ways.[3]

Understandably, eros has proved problematic or confusing in awakening traditions like Theravada Buddhism, which teach that the energies involved in sexual desire offer the illusory promise of fulfillment in the realm of the senses. In their view, this promise has the power to seduce practitioners (who are often young men) away from their spiritual vows and into a life exclusively focused on family, work, child-rearing, sickness, old age, and death. For this reason, sincere aspirants have generally been encouraged or required to renounce family ties, restrict or eliminate their contact with the opposite sex, take a vow of poverty and chastity, and enter a monastery or ashram where they can focus on spiritual practice.

Unfortunately, in their attempts to sublimate the power of eros and use it to fuel the practices of meditation and self-inquiry, these traditions have often tended to suppress it instead and encourage a kind of dualistic detachment and aversion, both to the beauty, joy, fullness, and vitality of the manifest world and to the ugliness and suffering it also inevitably entails. After all, since eros is more than just sexual attraction—it's the core life energy that courses through our bodies (synonymous with prana, Shakti, or kundalini)—and fuels the world of form, we attempt to suppress or sublimate it at our peril.

In my own experience as a monk in the Buddhist tradition, I saw the effects of such mixed messages about eros in the sexual acting-out of longtime practitioners and teachers who abused their power to seduce their students under the pretense of pure intentions and single-minded dedication to the teachings. Rather than embracing eros in a conscious and responsible way, they pretended to be too enlightened to have desires, while getting their sexual needs met in the shadows at the expense of others. (For more on the problem of teachers who go astray, see chapter 5, page 97.) At the other extreme, I remember early in my meditation practice meeting a renowned Burmese Buddhist master who seemed so detached and joyless that I questioned my desire to ordain as a monk. How, I wondered, could these energies be channeled in a healthy and life-affirming way?

From the nondual perspective, everything that arises in our experience is a complete and perfect expression of the mystery at the heart of reality. Our spiritual practice is to host the guests just as they are—the dark thought, the shame, the malice, the passionate attraction, the sexual longing—without attachment, identification, or rejection. As human beings in the world without recourse to a monastery or ashram to limit and circumscribe our expression, our lives inevitably involve eros in one form or another, and we can't ignore or transcend it.

When we attempt to embrace these powerful energies and turn intimate relationships into a process of deepening and embodying our awakening, however, we're forging our own path into uncharted terrain. The revered sages, rinpoches, and roshis of the past tended to be renunciates and yogis who have little to teach us today about the integration of realization back into the world of ordinary erotic human relationships. Instead, we need to rely on our own discoveries and the relational insights of Western psychology, which has been charting the complexities of intimacy since at least the time of Freud and his contemporaries. For us as laypeople, both awakening and its subsequent embodiment in time occurs and unfolds in the context of intimate relationships—with life, with other people, and with our loved ones in particular. And this journey would not be available to us without eros, embodied love and attachment.

The Higher and Lower Octaves of Love

One key to fully understanding and embracing these challenging energies is to regard love as a continuum from lower to higher octaves, with the nondual recognition that, as in a classical composition or a popular song, the higher notes are not superior to the lower. From this perspective, pure, selfless, unconditional love—involving the heart chakra and the upper energy centers of wisdom and self-realization—is the higher octave of the overarching energy of love, and eros is the lower octave, from the heart down through the centers that focus on interpersonal power, emotional attachment, sexual connection, and physical survival. The higher octave is more attuned to the absolute or essential level of reality and the lower octave with the relative, manifest level. But one is not better than the other (despite the associations with the words "higher" and "lower"), just as treble notes are not better than bass, and both are indispensable to living a fully engaged and embodied human life.

Admittedly, the higher octaves correspond with our notions of how spiritual people should behave—with wisdom, empathy, compassion, nonattachment, equanimity, and so forth—while the lower octaves can tend not only to provide pleasure, connection, and emotional fulfillment but also to be grasping (like an infant onto the mother, like lovers onto each other), voracious, aggressive, and attached to outcomes. But in the end, with the dawn of a more awakened, nondual understanding, the two octaves of love can be merged and reconciled in the heart. As suggested earlier, the way to reconcile them is to abide in our natural state of awake awareness and welcome and even enjoy whatever arises without attachment, identification, or rejection. This welcoming and all-embracing awareness is itself the "highest" octave of love, beyond dualistic distinctions of high and low.

Needless to say, we get glimpses of this merging of octaves in the dance of intimate relationships with romantic partners and family members, and especially in sexual union, when we share passionate, wholehearted, embodied love with our beloved. These are precious experiences of dimensions of interconnectedness beyond the ordinary and everyday. But like all experiences on the manifest level, they can't last but can only whet our appetites for nonseparation at every level. Genuine awakening is not about any experience, high or low, but about realizing ourselves as the experiencer, undisturbed by, and ultimately inseparable from, the so-called positive and negative experiences that inevitably arise.

Note: Some traditions, like Kundalini Yoga and nondual Shaiva Tantra, offer techniques for channeling the energy of the lower octaves through the chakras and out the crown of the head. In fact, hatha yoga was originally developed as a method for moving the energies of kundalini. But most of the authentic tantric lineages have died out, and the genuine, experienced teachers that remain are often reluctant to pass on their secret teachings and practices outside their cultural milieu. In any case, the tantric traditions of Buddhism and Hinduism are beyond the scope of this book, which focuses on the nondual pathless path teachings that I've studied and practiced.

Healthy Attachment and the Practice of Nonattachment

Most teachers and teachings in the nondual wisdom tradition recommend the attitude and practice of nonattachment as one of the cornerstones of the pathless path. We're advised to welcome our experience just as it is but without attachment or identification—or even more directly, we're pointed back to our natural state of awake awareness, which requires no practice and is always already unattached to what it's aware of.

In contemporary Western psychology, by contrast, the word "attachment" is used in a very different way, to describe an essential element in the process of human development. Studies have shown that a healthy, loving attachment to a consistently nurturing figure from the earliest moments of life is crucial to the emotional and even physical development of a growing child. As adults, our loving attachments to loved ones and friends are central to our survival and sense of security and give meaning and richness to our lives. No matter how awakened we may be, if we lose a parent, partner, or child, we experience grief in all its natural intensity. But here's the crucial distinction: We may grieve the loss but be unattached to the grief—and the more secure the attachment, the less attached we will be to the grief or any other human emotion.

Psychologists have found that human attachment can be either secure or insecure—with insecure attachment coming in three different varieties or flavors, depending on our experience with parents or other caregivers in childhood. Children who have generally been neglected or abandoned tend to develop avoidant attachment—that is, they avoid close relationships and try to be as self-sufficient as possible. Those who have received inconsistent parenting tend to be ambivalent, oscillating between holding on and pushing away. And children whose parents have been abusive or threatening learn to fear the person they're attached to, a style known as disorganized attachment. By contrast to these three forms of insecure attachment, children whose parents provide consistent love, care, and connection learn to trust the people who love them and feel little or no fear, avoidance, or ambivalence in relationships—in other words, they feel secure in their attachments.

These attachment styles have a profound influence on how we engage in intimate relationships because we tend to project our experience with early attachment figures onto our relationships with partners and other loved ones. Attachment is based on eros, broadly speaking, which is the energy that binds us and a core component of romantic and close familial relationships. Eros—passionate, vital, survival-level, lower-chakra love—is what connects us with the object of our attachment. As a result, insecure attachment gives relationships an added emotional charge as we struggle to avoid, manage, or maintain connection with a significant other we perceive to be threatening, rejecting, or inconsistent.

In practice, adults with insecure attachment—estimated to be about 40 percent of the US population[4]—find intimate relationships troubling, difficult, painful, or problematic to a greater or lesser degree. In fact, the combination of eros and insecure attachment in a single relationship creates a volatile mixture of powerful energies that may express themselves in passionate and even explosive ways. No wonder domestic violence is rampant and so many homicides in the United States occur between romantic partners. The more insecure the attachment, the more attached we are to having the attachment figure meet the needs we were never able to satisfy as children, and therefore the more demanding and controlling we will be.

But insecure attachment affects more than our relationships to other people; it affects our overall experience of life itself. In essence, we relate to the world, to everyday problems and life situations, as we do to our core attachment figures. If we attached insecurely to our caregivers, then we're going to feel insecure in the world, leading to a constant struggle to alleviate our insecurity. For example, we may limit our involvements in the world of work and career because we don't trust other people and prefer to make do on our own as much as we can (avoidant); we may wax hot and cold about our responsibilities and involvements, enthusiastic about work one week, then discouraged the next (ambivalent); or we may find ourselves constantly anxious about our ability to survive in a world that seems fragmented and out of control (disorganized).

In other words, much of the suffering and dissatisfaction we experience (what the Buddhists call *dukkha*) is caused by our sense of insecurity—feeling separate, alone, isolated, and unsupported in a hostile or withholding world. From this perspective, suffering is caused not by attachment, as the Buddhists suggest, but by insecure attachment. People who are securely attached tend to transfer this attachment to life itself and feel more secure, content, and peaceful—and experience less dukkha.

Ironically, if we're insecurely attached, we're more likely to try to force reality and other people to be different from the way they are, which is what attachment means in the Buddhist tradition. When we're securely attached we tend to feel safer and more sufficient, let go of trying to control every moment, and open more easily to the uncertainty of things as they are. As the Buddha said, happiness is wanting what you have and not wanting what you don't have.

Of course, insecure attachment may also motivate us to find a deeper source of security and satisfaction in that which cannot abandon, reject, disappoint, or abuse us—consciousness, spirit, buddha nature, awake awareness, true Self. As some people have discovered, awakening may be the ultimate cure for insecure attachment because it occasions a profound, unshakable, experiential recognition of our inseparability from the ground of Being—the matrix (from the Latin for "mother") out of which the manifest world arises. The great mother of the matrix can never abandon, confuse, or abuse us—she's ever present everywhere as the essence of existence itself. By attaching to the spiritual ground—from which, of course, we have never been separate, though it may have seemed so experientially—we can heal the wounds of insecure attachment, just as a strong and healthy adult relationship can.

This is not to say that those of us who are securely attached don't suffer for other reasons or are less inclined to seek spiritual realization. Suffering is endemic to the human condition, and the search for release from suffering is a timeless human endeavor. Besides, people seek enlightenment for a variety of reasons. However, the securely attached aren't looking to spirit to resolve core attachment issues—and so will be less inclined to attach themselves to the absolute and bypass the relative realm of ordinary, difficult human emotions.

Intimate Relationship as a Path of Awakening

Intimate interpersonal relationships offer a unique and powerful opportunity to live the dance of relationship in its broadest sense with a partner or a significant other. They provide a mirror of how and when we struggle, resist, and project onto reality, and a proving ground for working with and fine-tuning our fundamental relationship with life itself. At their most refined and mature, they can be a garden in which the pure and radiant love that we are—which may have first revealed itself in moments of spiritual insight or the initial flush of "being in love"—can root, grow, and flourish in our togetherness and expand outward to benefit all beings. At a more psychological level, such relationships offer a laboratory for resolving and healing the negative childhood conditioning, habitual reactive patterns, and insecure attachment issues that prevent us from abiding as the love that we are and keep driving us to seek our source of love in the arms of the other. Most of us tend to fluctuate between one scenario and the other, spending more and more time tending our garden only to fall back into the laboratory to do more experimenting and proving.

Some chroniclers of the spiritual journey make a distinction between the parallel tracks of waking up and growing up—realizing our timeless spiritual nature, on the one hand, and developing into a mature, loving, and fully functional human being in time, on the other. Intimate relationships offer an opportunity to work on both tracks at the same time, waking us up to our inherent inseparability while healing the wounds that keep us separate. For this reason, they're a powerful monastery or ashram in their own right. As one of my teachers used to say at the end of a long meditation retreat, "Now the real retreat begins."

Intimate relationships challenge our self-and-world construct system, the dualistic dream narrative of self and other, inside and outside, that perpetuates separation and keeps us from experiencing life as it is. Such relationships have the power in each moment to keep waking us up out of the dream into the reality of our interbeing (see chapter 6, page 119). Once we've glimpsed what it's like to live in the garden of undivided love with another, we can work with and release what gets in the way of doing it on a regular basis. In the process, we can release the conditioning of the past and expedite the process of growing beyond it. Of course, not every partner or close friend is available for this level of intimacy. In the end, ironically, the path of awakened relationship may be a largely solitary practice, a kind of ongoing, moment-to-moment meditation and self-inquiry, that leads to greater love and connectedness whether or not your partner deliberately participates.

Because they're so central to our well-being, intimate relationships invite us with unparalleled urgency to address the core questions of life: Can I remain open, loving, surrendered, and nonreactive in the midst of difficult negative emotions? Can I stay awake and communicate in ways that foster greater love and connectedness rather than conflict and division? And when I can't, how can I bring my deepest realization to bear to guide me home to awakened intimacy and nonseparation? As it goes in intimate relationships, so it follows in our relationships more broadly with the world inside and around us.

"A human being looking for love is like a wave in the ocean looking for water believing it's separate from water," writes the psychotherapist Lynn-Marie Lumiere. "In essence, we are the love we seek. Although it is inherent and already present as our own heart essence, it can be awakened in the presence of another. Awakened relating is about sharing and celebrating real love together, rather than trying to get it from each other. Once we know we are what we seek, it's possible to relate from a place of freedom, harmony, and acceptance, rather than from lack, grasping, and attachment."[5] This is the ideal and promise of awakened relationship.

Since most of the revered nondual masters of the past were yogis or renunciates or had traditional marriages with spouses who did not share their spiritual perspective, we don't have notable examples to consult for guidance on the journey of awakened relationship. Instead, we're forging our own unique synthesis of direct spiritual insight, nondual teachings, Western psychology, personal experience, and New Age techniques for encouraging intimacy to craft a thoroughly original and contemporary path. Though this evolving approach draws on both traditional meditation techniques and the interventions of relationship counseling, it's not primarily about methodology, it's about accessing the qualities and wisdom we already have and applying them to the journey of being together in a more awakened and nondual way in our complex and secular world.

Although I've worked with couples as a therapist for over thirty years and studied with some of the pioneers in the field, I certainly don't consider myself an expert on this topic, if indeed anyone possibly could be. But please allow me to offer some fundamental attitudes and commitments that I have found support the journey of awakened relating.[6]

Recognize that nothing outside you can provide lasting peace, happiness, and love. As long as you expect your partner to provide the love, fulfillment, support, and validation you so passionately crave, you'll be endlessly disappointed. Instead practice turning your finger back upon yourself and acknowledge that the only reliable source of love lies inside your own heart right now. Of course, those moments when we can share this love with another are especially precious—indeed, they're what draw and keep us together—but we can't expect our partner to meet us there whenever we want them to.

Return and rest as the love that you are as much as possible. In those moments of awakened awareness, or nondual presence, when all sense of separation momentarily falls away, you spontaneously touch the love that you are. Walking in nature, sitting quietly on your meditation cushion or chair, sharing togetherness with a loved one, you feel this pure, unconditional love move to the foreground unbidden. Hang out here as much as possible and let it fill and fulfill you. Another person is welcome, but not required.

Welcome yourself and your beloved as you are. Our natural state of nondual presence, awakened awareness, effortlessly welcomes what is because there's no separation between awareness and what it's aware of. This nonseparation is the source of universal and abiding love, which does not expect reality or the other person to be different from the way they are. Embracing your partner as they are, with an open heart born of awakened awareness, is a powerful and irreplaceable gift, especially since most of us didn't get this unconditional love and regard as children.

Tell the truth and let go of the illusion of control. Honesty in intimate relationships can be challenging because we believe that withholding what we're really thinking and feeling allows us to remain in control of the situation and the other person. But if you're genuinely committed to truth at every level, you'll feel moved to share your experience, surrender to the way it is, and let life naturally unfold in its own mysterious and uncontrollable way.

Communicate in ways that mirror your deepest truth. In the grip of strong emotions, we may revert to habitual ways of expressing ourselves with our partner that reflect a more dualistic worldview. Rather than the love and reconnection we really want, we end up triggering conflict, defensiveness, and division. Fortunately, there are forms of expression that teach us how to frame our communications in language that's specific, accurate, and respectful—in particular, the method known as nonviolent communication (NVC).

In NVC you learn to attune to your own feelings and those of your partner and express yourself honestly and authentically in language that's nonblaming. In this way, you invite empathy and connectedness with each other rather than conflict and polarization. As the communication unfolds, you end up feeling closer, and rigid positions and points of view begin to dissolve. In brief, the approach has four steps: Describe the situation as you see it (and stay open to the possibility that you may not see it accurately), express your feelings (while not implying that the other person is responsible for them), articulate the needs you would like to have met, and make a request that would meet your needs, resolve the conflict, and bring you closer again.[7]

If you're not fond of methodologies, a more direct, and therefore more challenging, approach would be to simply sit together and sense into your inseparability, or at least deep connection, in the heart. From this place, see if you can find the words that most accurately reflect your feelings and concerns. Before you begin speaking, notice how the words affect this deep connection. Do they cause your heart to contract or to open? Do they bring you closer or farther apart? Do they seem true or distorted in favor of your position? Do you sense that they open the possibility of resolving the issue or intensifying it? Take some time to find the best words, and begin your conversation, fine-tuning your communication as you go. (For a more nonverbal approach, see the meditation "Deepening the Connection with Affectionate Gazing" on page 219.)

Use relationships as an opportunity to wake up from the dream again and again. When you find yourself becoming reactive, pushing your point of view, or struggling with your partner, stop and become aware of the dream narrative you're projecting in this moment. What agenda are you attached to and why—and what's the self-and-world construct system on which it's based? The dream is often so familiar that we don't see it because it's the filter we're looking through, just as the eye can't see the eye. In a moment of clear seeing, you can relax your agenda, step out of the dream, and welcome the situation and your partner just as they are.

Return to wholeness by reclaiming the shadow. Jung believed that we inevitably project disowned and rejected parts of ourselves onto our significant other. In his view, the ongoing work of intimate relationships is to reclaim these shadow parts and integrate them into our larger sense of self, in a lifelong process known as individuation. The shadow has been a prominent topic in New Age and nondual circles in recent years amid claims that many people, including teachers, spiritually bypass their more human qualities and project them onto others. As described in the previous section, intimacy confronts us again and again with the inaccuracy of our projections and provides an excellent opportunity to own them as unacknowledged parts of ourselves and become more whole and complete at a relative level.

Embrace disappointment, it adds wood to the fire. Again, intimate relationships are inherently disappointing. They can't provide us with precisely the love and fulfillment we expect to receive—and for this very reason they add wood to the fire of the awakening process. If you view your relationships as an awakening journey rather than a source of personal gratification, you'll aways have plenty of fuel for the fire of awakening. From the spiritual perspective, as the Tibetan Buddhist teacher Chögyam Trungpa used to say, disappointment is extremely good news.

Reflect and Inquire

Spend some time reflecting on your most intimate relationship with a partner, lover, or other close friend or family member. If you don't have one currently, reflect on an intimate relationship you've had in the past. How would you assess the mix of the two octaves of love described in this chapter? If you experience emotional reactivity with this person from time to time, or often, ask yourself, what are the negative emotions that get triggered, and what are some of the interactions or circumstances that seem to trigger them? Needless to say, this is an emotionally fraught topic that may be difficult to address authentically, but do your best. How do I project my desires, expectations, and past conditioning onto this person and fail to see them as they are or understand their true intentions?

Do you experience moments of deep communion or even oneness with this person? Do you share a nondual spiritual perspective? If so, does it inform and deepen the relationship and help you get unhooked at the personal level of identity while meeting in the one heart you share? As Nisargadatta is quoted as saying, "The world is made of rings, the hooks are all yours. Let your hooks go, and nothing will hold you." What keeps you in this relationship even with its difficulties? What are the lessons you're learning? How does it inform and motivate your awakening journey? What else could you be doing to become more aware of your hooks and release their hold over you?

Q&A

Q: The use of the word "love" seems problematic to me. Perhaps I just have too many connotations with the word on the relative level to understand how it can be at the heart of the absolute level of being. I understand how there can be a fundamental sense of joy at the level of awareness, a delight in observing how the universe plays itself out. But love doesn't seem like the right word for it. Are there other words to use at that level?

A: In the early years of my spiritual journey, I couldn't understand how love entered into the awakening process either. I remember asking a fellow monk, echoing the song by Tina Turner, "What's love have to do with Zen?" But at a certain point my heart center opened wide, and I realized that love is the force that animates and connects us; it is the energy of interbeing. It's just another name or dimension of awakened awareness. They're inseparable. The emotion we call love is just the expression of this energy in the human heart. When you realize that the things and people around you are inseparable from you, love naturally arises and overflows.

Q: You mention the distinction between those who grieve the loss of a loved one while not awakened and those who grieve the loss from an awakened perspective. In the latter case, "we may grieve the loss but be unattached to the grief." What does this mean? How does it feel different? When I was faced with the loss of a young family member some years ago, my Zen teacher told me that it could act as a catalyst to my awakening. But this only made me angry, and I felt like I was grieving incorrectly.

A: Being unattached to grief, or any emotion, means welcoming it as it is but not feeding the stories that perpetuate it and turn pain into suffering. For example, "she died too young, life is unfair, I'll never be able to get over this loss," and so forth. Images and thoughts about this person may continue to arise spontaneously and elicit strong feelings, and grieving in this way can be a natural and appropriate way to honor and let go of the person you love. But don't hold on to the feelings, just welcome them, let them pass through, and eventually they will lose their hold over you. Host your emotions, as Rumi encouraged, but let them go when they're ready, and return and rest in awareness undisturbed.

Meditation: Deepening the Connection with Affectionate Gazing

You may live with a partner for years and share the most intimate moments, yet never spend long periods in silence together or dare to venture into uncharted terrain and gaze deeply into each other's eyes without the guardrails of words and concepts. What might you find if you stop and look? Who are you really, alone and together?

Schedule at least five minutes for this meditation. If you find it fruitful, you can do it again for ten minutes or longer.

Sit directly across from your partner with your eyes closed and knees almost touching. Spend a few moments relaxing and breathing together. You may never have gazed in this way before and so may be entering into new and uncertain terrain. Acknowledge any understandable fear or anxiety. Now open your eyes and begin gently gazing into each other's eyes.

Don't concentrate or focus your attention. Let your gaze be relaxed, soft, and affectionate. If you find yourself looking away, gently return to gazing again.

As you gaze, notice what thoughts and feelings arise. You may be concerned about how you look or about what your partner might see that they've never noticed before. You may be afraid of doing it wrong or of being judged as inadequate in some way. You may have a litany of self-judgments. Or you may be afraid that this gazing may evoke deeper feelings that you find uncomfortable.

At the same time, you may notice things in your partner's face and eyes that you hadn't noticed before. You may intuit feelings hiding beneath the surface that you hadn't been aware of, or their face may evoke feelings in you that you hadn't experienced: perhaps aversion or judgments you hadn't been aware of, or a level of affection or love you hadn't felt before. Unresolved issues and unexpressed feelings may come to the foreground that you want to share in future.

The face of your partner is like a mirror that reflects back to you the filter of ideas and projections through which you see them. Notice what you discover. No need to talk about anything now, just rest in the silence and continue your soft and affectionate gazing. If you find love arising in your heart, let it express itself through your eyes.

As you relax into the gazing, the thoughts and feelings may settle down, your partner's face may start to feel less solid, and you may sense a deeper current of love or interconnectedness. You may even feel the sense of separation between you dissolve and a new level of intimacy emerge. The one gazing and the one gazed at revealing themselves to be one and the same, a single awareness gazing out through different pairs of eyes.

Just continue gazing and welcoming what arises. Whatever comes, just take note of it as you continue your soft and affectionate gazing. When the meditation ends, appreciate each other for your willingness to venture into new territory together, and take some time to share and discuss what you experienced if you feel comfortable doing so.

10

Infinite Awakening, Endless Unfolding

Many people seem to be under the impression that spiritual awakening is a one-time occurrence that confers abiding and unshakable equanimity and freedom from all suffering on those who achieve it. In this view, once you've awakened to the nondual nature of reality, you should live, like Ramana Maharshi in his ashram in southern India, in the glow of selflessness ever after, no longer prone to the misguided narratives and reactive patterns of ego.

The fact is, for most people the initial awakening is just the first step on a lifelong journey of deepening, clarifying, and applying the awakened perspective to every circumstance we encounter. Rather than a one-and-done, we're constantly awakening and reawakening as we find ourselves getting lost in new dreams and identities, then seeing through them into new levels of clarity and freedom.

For this reason I titled the book *Infinite Awakening*, to dispel the errant notion that spiritual realization is a one-time shift in the locus of our identity and view of reality. Rather than a threshold we cross once and for all, awakening is a doorway into a radically different way of perceiving life that itself is constantly changing and evolving, moving to the foreground and then to the background again, or even going underground and being forgotten for a time until it resurfaces and reasserts its transformative power. (For a detailed map of the stages of awakening, see chapter 2.)

Infinite Awakening

Over the years I've taught intensive immersion programs, led embodiment groups, and had the opportunity to dialogue with thousands of seekers and bear witness to the infinite number of ways that awakening expresses itself. For most if not all of us, it encompasses a lifetime of approaching, glimpsing, forgetting, remembering, going deeper, getting lost, and finding our way again. Before we've even had a genuine breakthrough, or kensho, we go back and forth through a series of insights and openings that may take years to unfold.

Many of us spend years at the threshold, knocking on the door but finding our access blocked by a variety of factors beyond our control, including a lifetime of conditioning and reactivity, tenacious stories, memories, beliefs and expectations, the impact of trauma, and the conviction that awakening couldn't possibly happen for me. Once we've passed over the threshold, we may keep finding ourselves outside the doorway again, disoriented and not sure how to get back through. As a result, we keep returning to the teachers, teachings, and practices that help reorient and reawaken us on the endless journey of awakening and reawakening.

Once we've had genuine and lasting insights into the nondual nature of reality and our inherent lack of a permanent, abiding self, we may find that these insights don't consume our attachment, self-clinging, fear, anger, and delusion like a fire. Instead they flicker like a candle, never quite going out but never taking hold and replacing the old dream with clear seeing—that is, with a more accurate and awakened view of reality. We need to keep returning and reawakening until the glimpse blossoms into a fuller and more deeply rooted recognition that has the power to release the hold of the dream and transform our lives at every level.

The infinite and endless nature of awakening takes other forms as well. As our awakening unfolds and deepens and the light of awareness penetrates the darkest corners of our lives, we may find ourselves flooded with strong negative emotions and reactive patterns from the past that have lurked in the shadows and now have access to the light. Suddenly our precious peace of mind may be breached by old stories, memories, beliefs, and identities that we now need to see through and awaken from. For many people this ongoing process of recognizing and releasing, awakening and reawakening, can be unexpected and unsettling—and may last a lifetime.

Awakening tends to go through a series of predictable stages, as I describe in chapter 2, from more dualistic and superficial to more nondual and all-encompassing. Awakening also evolves through the energy centers of the body, and each new stage, though a natural denouement of the previous one, may feel like a powerful new revelation. For example, when your heart awakens, you may be flooded with a depth of love and compassion you've never experienced before, and you may feel overcome by the profound, joyful, and visceral knowing that you're not separate from the sun, sky, plants, animals, and people around you. Equally powerful and disorienting can be the awakening of the root chakra, as you find yourself falling into a groundless ground of emptiness and mystery. Each of these experiences constitutes a fresh awakening. In fact, every time we step out of the known into the unknown, we're awakening anew.

The human mind is a dream-making machine, offering up fresh points of view, interpretations, and perspectives for every new situation. But there is no awakened point of view—indeed, the infinite journey of awakening involves seeing through every point of view as it arises and returning to the openness and nonconclusion of don't-know mind. In the *Diamond Sutra*, so often cited in Zen, we're enjoined to "cultivate a mind that dwells nowhere"—or, in the words of my teacher Jean Klein, to keep opening to the openness beyond all knowing and points of view.

Just as reality itself is impermanent and ever-changing, so too are the mind-states and insights we've had over the years. But our true nature, our natural state of inherent wakefulness, does not go anywhere, even though it may fade into the background and elude our grasp. As Ramana Maharshi taught: Let what comes come. Let what goes go. Find out what remains. Of course, if we can't access our natural state, it's effectively unavailable and therefore doesn't exist for us right now, and each time we rediscover it may feel like a new awakening as well. Once we find our home ground of awakened awareness and take up our headquarters there, as the sage Nisargadatta Maharaj puts it, each moment offers yet another opportunity to see reality fresh and new from an awakened perspective, with awakened eyes and ears.

Endless Unfolding

In addition to the infinite awakening that continues to occur across a lifetime as the nondual nature of reality reveals itself again and again with increasing clarity and depth, there is the ongoing expression of this deeper truth in our everyday lives. How does the vertical, timeless, transcendent dimension of pure consciousness infuse and inform the dynamic, impermanent horizontal dimension of time and space? How does our awakened recognition of our boundless and compassionate spiritual nature manifest itself in the personal world of work and relationship? Now that we know that we're in essence not the fraction but the whole, not the wave but the ocean, do we feel more peace, happiness, and ease of being ourselves and treat other people with greater empathy and compassion, as one might expect? Or do we still get caught in self-centered thinking and try to impose our agenda on others? Now that we realize that we're not in charge of our lives but instead everything is taken care of by the sacred mystery, does our anxiety and fear dissolve into a deeper ground of trust in the unfolding? Or do we continue to struggle with the present and worry about the future? If awakening doesn't relieve our suffering and reduce our reactivity, what value does it have for us, our loved ones, and the broader world in general?

The integration of our awakened understanding in everyday life is sometimes called embodiment, or waking down. After we've awakened to our "higher" spiritual nature, how do we wake down and in to the minute particulars of everyday life—cooking a meal, driving in traffic, discussing politics with a neighbor, interacting with a sales representative on the phone, cheering for our favorite team? Where's our precious realization of our interconnectedness and interbeing in moments like those? How thoroughly do we embody, or give expression to, the truths we've recognized so far only in meditation or self-inquiry?

The term "embodiment" may suggest that we're trying to pack certain qualities and values into this separate being of flesh and blood, but in fact it's quite the opposite. The less we identify with the body and mind or take ownership of the thoughts and feelings that inevitably arise, the more we give living expression to the ineffable and universal essence of our being and allow spirit to move through us. The challenge is: How do we meet the messy particulars of everyday life through this imperfect human form, infused and inspired by our deep recognition of the sacred perfection at the heart of reality? How do we let go of ego's need to hold on to control and allow ourselves to be moved by the natural flow of life?

Awakened living is not a self-improvement project and has nothing to do with being perfect or doing it right according to some predetermined ideal. To the contrary, it's about letting go of trying to get yourself and life to be a certain way and welcoming reality just as it is, in all its (innately perfect) imperfection. Any attempt to judge how you're doing just takes you away from the mystery and spontaneity of living in the ungraspable now. You know you're moving into alignment with the deeper truth of your being when you're no longer the center of your life or the primary focus of your thinking, you're following the movement of life rather than struggling to control it, you feel greater intimacy with what is, and you experience more and more moments of ease, peace, trust, openness, and gratitude for this precious human incarnation.

Paradoxically, letting go of your ongoing attempts to be a perfect, awakened, spiritual person releases you to be who you actually are at every level and to give expression to the unique gifts you were born to contribute on this horizontal human plane. Free of ideas of how awakened behavior is supposed to look, you can act spontaneously and authentically, from a place of wholeness rather than division, interbeing rather than separation. Indeed, a sense of authenticity may be the clearest indication that you're living in alignment with the deeper truth of your being—or even more accurately, the deeper truth of Being itself. The famous teaching of Ramana Maharshi echoes here: To remain as you are, without question or doubt, is your natural state—and the source of all authentic and appropriate action.

Not surprisingly, given that you're on the pathless path, there are no prescribed methods for living in alignment, except to keep reorienting to the awakened view and allow it to inform every moment. For this, the simple practice of the four Rs—remember to reorient, recognize your natural state of awakened awareness, return, and rest there—can be quite effective. (For detailed instructions, see 131.) Another powerful pointer from Ramana: Immerse yourself in the living present and don't worry about the future. The future will take care of itself. That is, let go of trying to plan or figure things out with the mind. Instead, be intimate with the way things are right now and allow the natural and spontaneous movement of life to carry you along in its flow.

With his characteristically sharp sword and a touch of wry humor, the sage Nisargadatta Maharaj cuts through all the deliberations of the mind with this simple recommendation: Do it if you're doing it, don't do it if you're not doing it. In other words, no matter what you do, you're an instrument of the divine and you need merely trust what is already spontaneously unfolding through you. Perhaps not surprisingly, neuroscience backs up this view. According to research, the neurological impulse to take a certain action arises a second or two before the decision to act has consciously occurred. That is, you're already doing what you're doing before you decide to do it.

Here are a few more helpful guidelines for aligning your words and actions with your deeper knowing:

- Keep returning to recognize and rest in your natural state, prior to thought, the boundaryless openness that's always already present. Don't jump to interpretations or conclusions. Remain in the silent presence of not knowing, and allow words and actions to arise from here.
- Identify and let go of any preconceptions or expectations you bring to the current situation, and refrain from drawing conclusions. Welcome the way things are wholeheartedly, without interpretation, and ask yourself not what do *I* want to happen here, but what does life want to happen through me? How does love want to respond right now? As Ramana has said, do what feels right in a given moment, then leave it behind.
- Remember that you're not the fraction but the whole, not the wave but the ocean. Attune to the natural movement and flow of the vast ocean of being rather than the erratic and impulsive shifts and changes of ego. Ask yourself, how can I align with the deeper direction for the collective benefit of the whole?

Attuning in this way to the natural flow of life, rather than contracting around a particular agenda or projected outcome, means letting go of the goal orientation we've been trained to cultivate and maintain since childhood. In the developed nations of the West at least, we're taught to glorify the fraction, the individual and their accomplishments, and deemphasize or even ignore the whole, the collective movement for the benefit of all. From school age onward, we're pressured to accomplish, make our mark, establish our position, strive to stay ahead, and prove our worth, as if we weren't inherently worthy. The ruling archetype is the hero, who succeeds with superhuman effort in the battle against the overwhelming forces arrayed before him. In this paradigm, surrendering to the flow of life is not even a viable option. No wonder our attempts to be authentic and align with the deeper flow inevitably prove to be imperfect, informed as they are by a lifetime of cultural conditioning. In this phase of the pathless path, as in every other, we need to be kind and compassionate with ourselves.

Not Knowing Is the Most Intimate

In essence, the path of authentic embodiment involves waking up from the dream we've constructed moment after moment and living in the unknowable and unpredictable now, as Ramana suggests. Awakened life naturally follows as we stay true to who we really are and free, as much as possible, from identification with the beliefs and stories that make up the dream narrative. It's the opposite of the hero's journey—being lived rather than imposing our agenda; letting go and letting God, as they say in the twelve-step movement, rather than leading the charge; being a servant of life rather than its imaginary master. Asking not what do I want, but what does the moment, reality, the whole, want from me?

At the deepest and most existential level, each moment itself is a new revelation, unlike any moment that's ever come before. Now the mystery is expressing itself like this, and now like this, and our purpose as consciousness in human form is to bear grateful witness to the sacred miracle of each fresh arising. One of my breakthrough realizations in a lifetime of endless awakenings was the recognition that continuity is ultimately an illusion perpetuated by the mind, and manifest reality arises fresh out of the depths of the unmanifest mystery moment after moment—in other words, in the timeless Now. In fact, time itself is a mystery, and there is only Now, endlessly changing and unfolding and giving the appearance of time passing.

Finally, the journey of awakening and embodiment is inevitably infinite and endless because countless beings are still lost in the suffering and confusion of the dream and long for freedom. Our job as bodhisattvas, those whose lives are dedicated to awakening, is to keep offering the possibility of awakening to all who seek it. In these perilous times, when human beings seem poised on the brink of collective annihilation, awakening to our inseparability, our interbeing, may be the only way through. In the words of the four vows of Zen:

> Sentient beings are numberless, I vow to guide them to liberation.
> Delusions are inexhaustible, I vow to reveal and release them.
> Reality is mysterious, I vow to appreciate it fully.
> The way of awakening is unsurpassable, I vow to embody it.

Or the loving-kindness meditation of the Theravada Buddhist tradition:

> May all beings be happy. May all beings be peaceful. May all beings be free from suffering. May all beings realize the love and light of our essential nature.

Meditation: Into the Mystery

When we recognize the nondual nature of reality, we realize that what's gazing out through these eyes is not separate from what it's gazing at. Subject and object, inside and outside, self and other, are not two; they're expressions of the same aware essence.

But beyond the realm of experience, these insights and distinctions drop away into the sacred mystery beyond all knowing or recognition. This is the dimension of pure consciousness, the One without a second, the groundless ground, which is unknowable even to the subtlest form of knowing. It knows itself by itself; it is its own knowing.

You can never really know it, you can only be it.

Since this dimension can't be experienced, it's often turned into an object of veneration or worship. The peace that surpasses all understanding. The holy spirit. Ayn sof. The dharmakaya. The ultimate reality prior to all manifestation.

In this more advanced meditation, you'll have an opportunity to taste this ultimate reality, the groundless ground beyond all knowing, where all distinctions, identities, and self fall away.

Begin by sitting quietly with your eyes open and look at the objects around you in the usual way. Notice the window, the table, the chair, the lamp.

Drop the names and concepts as much as possible and just look without interpretation.

Now shift your way of looking, and notice—or at least consider the possibility—that the one looking out through these eyes and what's being looked at are not separate.

The space between is only a construct, and the looker and what is looked at are interconnected and made of the same Being, the same empty essence.

Gazing with sheer awareness into sheer awareness, as a Buddhist teaching puts it.

If this doesn't make any sense to you right now, don't worry, you might like to go back and first read the meditation "Waking into the Nondual" on page 43.

Now let go of even this insight into the nondual nature of reality and let your looking be innocent and nonconceptual. Dual, nondual, none of it makes any sense right now. You don't know what a single thing is.

There is only direct perception, without any conceptual overlay. Just this, the limitless Now, expressing itself in a multiplicity of forms.

Now allow your awareness to slowly drop down from your head into your heart, and then through the heart center down through the floor into the depths of Being.

Into a groundless ground of silence and stillness prior to all sound and activity.

Into an ocean of Being and timeless Presence, prior to any individual awareness.

Into a deep reservoir of infinite potential, prior to all manifestation.

Into the Mystery, the One without a second, prior to all knowing.

It's like falling through space without a parachute, knowing that there's no ground to break your fall and no need for fear or concern. In fact, you are the very space through which you seem to be falling.

These may only be words at first, but let them guide you into this infinite and nonlocalizable dimension of being, the groundless ground, the empty source and essence of all manifestation.

Let go of all control and all knowing. Allow reality to take care of itself.

No guardrails, nothing to hold on to, no place to land, nothing to fear.

No danger, no problems, no stories, no separation, no *self*.

Just endlessly falling through the boundless openness that you really are.

Continue to let go into the groundless ground for as long as you like.

When you feel complete, open your eyes, get up, and go about your day, and notice how your experience of reality has changed.

Acknowledgments

Many years ago, when I lived on the island of Kaua'i, I happened upon this saying scrawled on an outhouse wall: "That which you are seeking is always seeking you." I often quote it when I teach, because it reminds us of who's really in charge of the search.

I bow with utmost reverence to the One without a second, which is always seeking you and me, not with any effort, intention, or deliberation, but because truth naturally seeks to recognize, reveal, and delight in itself whenever it can. As my beloved teacher Jean Klein used to say, the seeker is the sought, the looker is what he or she is looking for. We sense it in each moment, beckoning to us to step out of the illusory dream of the mind's devising and fall into the silent mystery, the vast ocean of being out of which this tiny wave is endlessly arising.

I bow with inexpressible gratitude to those who have pointed me again and again to who I really am with the patience, love, and wisdom of those who know and seek to share it—especially, to Shunryu Suzuki Roshi, Kobun Chino, Jean Klein, Tsoknyi Rinpoche, Byron Katie, and Adyashanti—and to the friends and colleagues who have shared the teaching path with me, especially John Prendergast, Dorothy Hunt, Yeshe Grant, Palden Drolma, Loch Kelly, and Suzanne Segal.

I bow with wonder and delight to my students, whose devotion to truth is a source of ongoing inspiration for me and whose hunger for clear and compassionate guidance motivates me to deepen and expand my own realization for their benefit and to find fresh ways to articulate the ineffable.

Finally, I bow with deep appreciation to the folks at Shambhala, itself one of the Dharma treasures in the West, for choosing to publish and promote this distinctly nontraditional book—and especially to Jenn Brown, my editor and champion, who chose it and guided it lovingly through the editorial process to become the finished volume you hold in your hands.

To be alive in this timeless and irreplaceable moment is the most precious gift. May you find in these pages the guidance to receive and treasure it!

Notes

Introduction

1 T. S. Eliot, *Four Quartets: A Poem* (HarperCollins, 2014).

Chapter One: What Does Spiritual Awakening Really Mean?

1 Sri Nisargadatta Maharaj, *I Am That* (Chetana Publishing, 1999).
2 Eckhart von Hochheim (Meister Eckhart), "True Hearing," trans. Claud Field M.A. (1909).
3 The Indian-American Hindu guru Paramahansa Yogananda, author of the spiritual classic *Autobiography of a Yogi* and founder of the Self-Realization Fellowship, claimed that secret Tibetan texts chronicled Jesus's fourteen years of study among saints and sages in India and regions of the Himalayas. For more information, see https://yoganandasite.wordpress.com/2017/06/30/the-unknown-years-of-jesus-life-sojourn-in-india-yogananda-and-jesus/.
4 It can be difficult to find therapists experienced in dealing with the psychological issues of meditation and spiritual awakening, but it's well worth a thorough search online, especially since many therapists now offer virtual sessions. Modalities that are particularly well suited to this kind of work include EMDR, internal

family systems (IFS), and body-based therapies that include somatic experience as well as conceptual thought.

Chapter Two: The Stages of Awakening

1 The ten oxherding pictures are a popular series of short poems and accompanying drawings used in the Zen tradition to describe the stages of a practitioner's journey to awakening and back to living an awakened life for the benefit of others. For one popular version, see *Zen Flesh, Zen Bones: A Collection of Zen & Pre-Zen Writings*, comp. Paul Reps and Nyogen Sanzaki (Tuttle Publishing, 1998).

2 The *Genjokoan* is widely considered to be one of the core texts of Japanese Zen, and there are numerous English translations that differ quite significantly from one another. Indeed, some scholars consider these teachings to be untranslatable. This version is my own, based on several of the most popular renditions, as are subsequent quotes from Dogen.

3 Lex Hixon, *Mother of the Buddhas: Meditation on the Prajnaparamita Sutra* (Quest Books, 1993).

4 Jean Klein, *I Am* (New Sarum Press, 2021), 41.

5 John Welwood, *Toward a Psychology of Awakening: Buddhism, Psychotherapy, and the Path of Personal and Spiritual Transformation* (Shambhala Publications, 2002).

6 For more information on the three points or stages of Garab Dorje, including the original text, see https://www.lotsawahouse.org/indian-masters/garab-dorje/three-statements-that-strike-vital-point.

7 Dzigar Kongtrul Rinpoche, *Peaceful Heart: The Buddhist Practice of Patience* (Shambhala Publications, 2020).

Chapter Four: The Direct Approach

1 Bodhidharma is an Indian or southwest Asian master who is traditionally regarded as the one who brought Zen (Chan) to China in the

fifth or sixth century B.C.E. Various teachings and legendary events are attributed to him, but little is known of his actual origin or activity. For more information see https://encyclopediaofbuddhism.org/wiki/Bodhidharma.

2 Philip Yampolsky, trans., *The Platform Sutra of the Sixth Patriarch* (Columbia University Press, 2012), 130.

3 Yampolsky, *The Platform Sutra of the Sixth Patriarch*, 132.

4 The story goes like this: A university professor visits a Zen master, and the master offers to pour the professor tea. As he holds out his cup, the professor continues to ply the master with intellectual questions. When the cup overflows and burns his fingers, the teacher cries out in shock and pain. "What are you doing? The cup is overfull, no more tea will go in." "Like this cup," the master replies, "you are full of your own opinions and speculations. How can I show you Zen unless you first empty your cup?" See https://www.lajosbrons.net/blog/nan-in-and-the-professor-a-western-zen-parable/#easy-footnote-bottom-1-82.

5 Shunryū Suzuki, *Branching Streams Flow in the Darkness: Zen Talks on the Sandokai,* ed. Mel Weitsman and Michael Wenger (University of California Press, 1999).

6 Chögyam Trungpa, "The Everyday Practice," n.d., Christopher Sunyata, https://sunyata.info/everyday-practice.

7 Yongey Mingyur Rinpoche, "Non-Meditation and Non-Distraction: Meditation," December 21, 2017, https://www.youtube.com/watch?v=wVRdESC3DN4.

8 Roshi Joan Halifax, "On Zazen—by Roshi Joan Halifax," July 22, 2024, Upaya Zen Center, https://www.upaya.org/2024/07/on-zazen-by-roshi-joan-halifax/.

9 David Godman, "The Practice of Self-Enquiry," July 12, 2019, David Godman, https://www.davidgodman.org/the-practice-of-self-enquiry/.

10 Shunryu Suzuki, *Zen Mind, Beginner's Mind: Informal Talks on Zen Meditation and Practice* (Shambhala Publications, 2011).

11 Seung Sahn, *Only Don't Know: Selected Teaching Letters of Zen Master Seung Sahn*, ed. Hyon Gak (Shambhala Publications, 1999).

Chapter Five: Why Bother with a Teacher?

1 For more information on the "special transmission," see the section "Direct Pointing and Special Transmission in Zen" on page 70.
2 I explore this topic at length in an article I wrote in 2006 for *Tricycle: The Buddhist Review* titled "In the Shadow of the Dharma." The article, originally accepted but never published, is now available as a blog entry on my website: https://stephanbodian.org/2019/12/4/in-the-shadow-of-the-dharma.
3 Welwood, *Toward a Psychology of Awakening*.

Chapter Six: Deconstructing the Dream

1 For more on Bugental's understanding of the self-and-world construct system, see this excerpt from his book *Psychotherapy Isn't What You Think: Bringing the Psychotherapeutic Engagement into the Living Moment*, n.d., https://www.psychotherapy.net/article/bugental.
2 Thomas Metzinger, *The Ego Tunnel: The Science of the Mind and the Myth of the Self* (Basic Books, 2009), 29.
3 Sanaz Talaifar and William Swann, "Self and Identity," *Oxford Research Encyclopedia of Psychology*, March 28, 2018, https://doi.org/10.1093/acrefore/9780190236557.013.242.
4 William Shakespeare, *Macbeth* (Turtleback Books, 1993), act 5, scene 5.
5 Translation by the author, *The Dhammapada*, verses 153–54.
6 William Wordsworth, *Ode: Intimations of Immortality from Recollections of Early Childhood* (Kessinger Publishing 2010).
7 From the song "Conductor" by Jai Uttal. Used with permission of the songwriter.

8 Ṭhānissaro Bhikkhu, "The Wisdom of the Ego," Dharma talk, n.d., https://www.dhammatalks.org/books/Head&HeartTogether/Section0012.html.

Chapter Seven: Welcoming What Is

1 Seng-ts'an, *Hsin-Hsin Ming: Verses on the Faith-Mind*, trans. Richard Clark (White Pine Press, 2001), 7. Used by permission of the publisher.
2 From *The Essential Rumi*, trans. Coleman Barks (HarperCollins, 2004), 109. Used by permission of the translator.
3 Seng-ts'an, *Hsin-Hsin Ming*, 7.
4 "The Host and Guest—From The Surangama Sutra," *Buddhism Now*, September 28, 2018, https://buddhismnow.com/2018/09/28/the-host-and-guest-from-the-surangama-sutra/.
5 Hixon, *Mother of the Buddhas*, 1993), 247.
6 Tara Brach, *Radical Compassion: Learning to Love Yourself and Your World with the Practice of RAIN* (Random House, 2020).
7 For complete instructions on practicing both long and short forms of tonglen, see Lama Palden Drolma, *Love on Every Breath: Tonglen Meditation for Transforming Pain into Joy* (New World Library, 2019).
8 Richard Schwartz, *No Bad Parts: Healing Trauma and Restoring Wholeness with the Internal Family Systems Model* (Sounds True, 2021), 16.
9 Seng-ts'an, *Hsin-Hsin Ming*, 7.
10 Seng-ts'an, *Hsin-Hsin Ming*, 12.

Chapter Eight: The Impact of Trauma

1 For extensive instructions in extending love and compassion to yourself and others, consider Tara Brach, *Radical Acceptance: Embracing Your Life with the Heart of a Buddha* (Bantam, 2004); and

Sharon Salzberg, *Lovingkindness: The Revolutionary Art of Happiness* (Shambhala, 2002).

Chapter Nine: Awakening Relationship

1 Janey Davies, "The Human Heart Has a Mind of Its Own, Scientists Find," *Learning Mind,* September 16, 2016, https://www.learning-mind.com/the-human-heart-mind/.

2 Seng-ts'an, *Hsin-Hsin Ming,* 12.

3 Stephan Bodian, "In The Shadow of the Dharma: Why Buddhist Teachers Have Sex with Their Students—and What We Can Do About It," December 4, 2019, https://www.stephanbodian.org/blog/2019/12/4/in-the-shadow-of-the-dharma.

4 Loren Soeiro, "What Does It Mean to Have an Insecure Attachment Style?," *Psychology Today,* January 29, 2020, https://www.psychologytoday.com/us/blog/i-hear-you/202001/what-does-it-mean-have-insecure-attachment-style?eml.

5 Lynn Marie Lumiere, *Awakened Relating: A Guide to Embodying Undivided Love in Intimate Relationships* (New Harbinger, 2018), 367.

6 For more in-depth exploration of the path of awakened relationship, see the work of C. G. Jung, John Welwood, Byron Katie Mitchell, Gay and Kathlyn Hendricks, A. H. Almaas, Stephen and Ondrea Levine, and Lynn Marie Lumiere. Other authors whose work in the field of psychology supports conscious and compassionate relating include Marshall Rosenberg, John Gottman, Sue Johnson, Harville Hendrix, and Stan Tatkin.

7 Marshall B. Rosenberg, *Nonviolent Communication: A Language of Life: Life-Changing Tools for Healthy Relationships* (PuddleDancer Press, 2015).

Additional Resources

Adyashanti, *Emptiness Dancing*. Sounds True, 2009.

Adyashanti, *The Way of Liberation: A Practical Guide to Spiritual Enlightenment*. Open Gate Sangha, 2013.

Aitken, Robert. *Taking the Path of Zen*. North Point Press, 2015.

Aitken, Robert. *The Mind of Clover: Essays in Zen Buddhist Ethics.* North Point Press, 1984.

Armstrong, Guy. *Emptiness: A Practical Guide for Meditators*. Wisdom Publications, 2017.

Balsekar, Ramesh S. *Pointers from Nisargadatta Maharaj*. Lotus Prints, 2024.

Beck, Charlotte Joko. *Ordinary Wonder: Zen Life and Practice*. Shambhala Publications, 2021.

Bodian, Stephan. *Wake Up Now: A Guide to the Journey of Spiritual Awakening*. McGraw Hill, 2010.

Bodian, Stephan. *Beyond Mindfulness: The Direct Approach to Lasting Peace, Happiness and Love.* New Harbinger, 2017.

Brach, Tara. *True Refuge: Finding Peace and Freedom in Your Own Awakened Heart*. Bantam, 2016.

Carse, David. *Perfect Brilliant Stillness.* Paragate Publishing, 2005.

Chödrön, Pema. *When Things Fall Apart: Heart Advice for Difficult Times*. Shambhala Publications, 2000.

Drolma, Lama Palden. *Love on Every Breath: Tonglen Meditation for Transforming Pain into Joy*. New World Library, 2018.

Harris, Sam. *Waking Up: A Guide to Spirituality Without Religion*. Simon and Schuster, 2015.

Hunt, Dorothy. *Ending the Search: From Spiritual Ambition to the Heart of Awareness*. Sounds True, 2018.

Katie, Byron, and Stephen Mitchell. *A Mind at Home with Itself: How Asking Four Questions Can Free Your Mind, Open Your Heart, and Turn Your World Around*. HarperOne, 2017.

Kelly, Loch. *The Way of Effortless Mindfulness: A Revolutionary Guide for Living an Awakened Life*. Sounds True, 2019.

Khenchen Thrangu Rinpoche. *Essentials of Mahamudra: Looking Directly at the Mind*. Wisdom Publications, 1996.

Khenpo, Nyoshul, and Surya Das. *Natural Great Perfection: Dzogchen Teachings and Vajra Songs*. Snow Lion, 2009.

Klein, Jean. *I Am*. New Sarum Press, 2021.

Klein, Jean. *Transmission of the Flame*. New Sarum Press, 2020.

Loy, David. *Nonduality: In Buddhism and Beyond*. Simon and Schuster, 2019.

Lumiere, Lynn Marie. *Awakened Relating: A Guide to Embodying Undivided Love in Intimate Relationships*. New Harbinger, 2018.

Maharaj, Sri Nisdargadatta. *I Am That*. Chetana Publishing, 1999.

Maharshi, Ramana. *Be as You Are: The Teachings of Sri Ramana Maharshi*. Edited by David Godman. Penguin UK, 1989)

Maharshi, Ramana. *The Teachings of Ramana Maharshi*. Edited by Arthur Osborne. Random House, 2014.

Pine, Red. *Three Zen Sutras: The Heart Sutra, The Diamond Sutra, and The Platform Sutra*. Catapult, 2021.

Poonja, H. W. L. *Wake Up and Roar*. Sounds True, 2007.

Prendergast, John J. *The Deep Heart: Our Portal to Presence*. Sounds True, 2019.

Reps, Paul, and Nyogen Senzaki, comps.. *Zen Flesh, Zen Bones: A Collection of Zen and Pre-Zen Writings*. Tuttle Publishing, 1998.

Salzberg, Sharon. *Lovingkindness: The Revolutionary Art of Happiness.* Shambhala Publications, 2020.

Schwartz, Richard. *No Bad Parts: Healing Trauma and Restoring Wholeness with the Internal Family Systems Model.* Sounds True, 2021.

Spira, Rupert. *The Nature of Consciousness: Essays on the Unity of Mind and Matter.* Sahaja, 2017.

Suzuki, Shunryu. *Branching Streams Flow in the Darkness: Zen Talks on the Sandokai.* Edited by Mel Weitsman and Michael Wenger. University of California Press, 2001.

Suzuki, Shunryu. *Zen Mind, Beginner's Mind.* Shambhala Publications, 2020.

van der Kolk, Bessel. *The Body Keeps the Score: Brain, Mind, and Body in the Healing of Trauma.* Penguin Books, 2014.

Wallis, Christopher. *Tantra Illuminated: The Philosophy, History, and Practice of a Timeless Tradition.* Mattamayura Press, 2013.

Welwood, John. *Toward a Psychology of Awakening: Buddhism, Psychotherapy, and the Path of Personal and Spiritual Transformation.* Shambhala Publications, 2002.

Yongey Mingyur Rinpoche and Helen Tworkov. *In Love with the World: A Monk's Journey Through the Bardos of Living and Dying.* Random House, 2021.

About the Author

Stephan Bodian is a teacher in the nondual wisdom tradition of Zen, Dzogchen, and Advaita Vedanta. Trained as a Buddhist monk for ten years, he had the good fortune to study with some of the great masters of our time, including Shunryu Suzuki Roshi, author of *Zen Mind, Beginner's Mind*; Advaita master Jean Klein, author of *I Am* and *Transmission of the Flame*; and Adyashanti, from whom he received Dharma transmission (authorization to teach) in 2001. After practicing as a monastic, Stephan trained as a psychotherapist (and now offers spiritual counseling) because he feels that Western psychology has important insights to share that complement the fundamental teachings and practices of the nondual traditions of the East. Since 2007 he has taught an intensive, full-immersion program in nondual wisdom known as the School for Awakening. His other books include *Meditation for Dummies, Buddhism for Dummies, Wake Up Now*, and *Beyond Mindfulness*.